PLANTS

OF ROCKY MOUNTAIN
NATIONAL PARK

by RUTH ASHTON NELSON

with assistance from
BEATRICE E. WILLARD

D1557095

With Color Illustrations and Keys for Identification

Published by the

ROCKY MOUNTAIN NATURE ASSOCIATION, INC.

in cooperation with the

NATIONAL PARK SERVICE,
U.S. DEPARTMENT OF THE INTERIOR

The Rocky Mountain Nature Association, Inc., is
a nonprofit organization cooperating with the
National Park Service in the interpretation and
management of Rocky Mountain National Park.

Contents

It is gratifying to observe the usefulness of previous editions of Mrs. Nelson's book. I hope that this popular version will continue to direct attention to the beauty of a wildflower. But each flower is more than a thing of beauty, and Ruth Nelson, in this continued labor of love, offers a simple explanation of the value and purpose of a healthy environment. I am certain that this edition will continue to direct attention upon Rocky Mountain wildflowers, but it will also help develop a better understanding of our precious environmental heritage.

TOM D. THOMAS
Chief Park Naturalist
Rock Mountain National Park

Foreword

For many people one of the most delightful experiences of a visit to Rocky Mountain National Park is the discovery of nature's wildflower gardens. Unlike the formal plantings at home, the unplanned orderliness of either a single blossom or the carpet of color in a meadow adds new zest and pleasure to any visitor's trip.

As a child, Mrs. Ruth Ashton Nelson's love for wildflowers was stimulated by summers spent in the high Rockies. This love continued to grow with her permanent residence in the area. Her desire to share this pleasure with friend and stranger culminated in the first edition of her book, *Plants of Rocky Mountain National Park,* published by the Government Printing Office in 1933. A revised edition was printed in 1953.

This third edition, in full color, is the result of much additional study and field work by Mrs. Nelson and others and reflects the benefit of her collaboration with her late husband, the eminent Dr. Aven Nelson, dean of Rocky Mountain botanists. Her skill in noting and describing salient field characteristics as guides to plant identification makes her work especially valuable to the observant but untrained person interested in flowers and plants. The effectiveness of the key to identification makes the book a valuable asset in the university classroom as well as to the amateur botanist.

Dr. Bettie Willard of the Thorne Ecological Foundation collaborated with Mrs. Nelson to bring the most accurate possible listing of all plants in Rocky Mountain National Park.

The National Park Service is genuinely pleased to have obtained the services of the author of the original editions for the preparation of this revision published by the Rocky Mountain Nature Association. It will assure the visitors to Rocky Mountain National Park a work which will add greatly to their understanding and enjoyment of this magnificent area.

GEORGE B. HARTZOG, JR.
Director - 1970
National Park Service

This 1976 reprint merely updates the book and makes minor corrections.

Preface

This book is based on three earlier editions of *Plants of Rocky Mountain National Park,* plus some new material. The original edition was published in 1933 by the U.S. Government Printing Office, and it proved to be so popular that it was revised in 1953 and 1970.

When the first edition was in preparation 40 years ago, the standard manuals on plant identification for this area were *New Manual of Botany of the Central Rocky Mountains* by John M. Coulter, revised by Aven Nelson, and *Flora of the Rocky Mountains and Adjacent Plains* by P. A. Rydberg. Both of these books have long been out of print.

During the past years, botanists have been revising the families and genera embracing a large number of plants. Within this time, botanical concepts and methods of systematic treatment of plant entities have undergone considerable change. In 1954, Sage Books published *Manual of the Plants of Colorado* by H. D. Harrington. This is an exhaustive treatment of all plants known to grow in the State and is basic for botanical study in this area. In 1953, the University of Colorado published a *Handbook of Plants of the Colorado Front Range* by William A. Weber. This book, revised in 1961 and again in 1967 and 1972, is called *A Rocky Mountain Flora.* I is less technical than the publications by Harrington, is well illustrated with excellent line drawings, and is very useful for the area it covers, which includes the eastern slope of Rocky Mountain National Park.

In the main, the author has endeavored to follow these recent treatments, still keeping in mind the original goal of offering a practical method of wildflower identification for nature lovers. Many of the Latin names used in this edition differ from those in earlier editions. One reason for changing these names is that, in many cases, extensive research revealed an earlier valid name of the species. Another is the current tendency to reduce closely related entities to one species and designate the differing forms as subspecies or varieties. Some common names used in earlier editions have been omitted or changed to bring them into agreement with modern popular usage. All authors' names have been omitted because it is believed that they are not meaningful to most users of this book. Botanists who wish to know these names will be able to find them by referring to either the Harrington or Weber publication. In most cases, if the name used here differs from the one given in one of these publications, the latter will be given as a synonym.

The first edition of this publication was based on research done in connection with work for a master of science degree at the Botany Department at Colorado Agricultural and Mechanical College, now Colorado State University. Since then, the author has done much additional field work in the park and has been continuously alert for new information regarding the plantlife of this area. Several eminent botanists gave valuable suggestions and assistance in connection with the preparation of the earlier editions, especially the late Dr. Aven Nelson, the late Dr. H. C. Hanson, and Dr. L. W. Durrell. More recently, Dr. William A. Weber, Curator of the Herbarium at the University of Colorado, and Dr. C. L. Porter, recently retired Curator of the Rocky Mountain Herbarium at the University of Wyoming, have been very generous and helpful. Other botanists have carried on valuable research in the park, which has contributed to knowledge of the plants.

Extensive, valuable collecting was done on the western slope of the Continental Divide, especially in the Never Summer Range, both within and just outside the park boundary by John and Margaret Douglass during the summers of 1959, 1960, and 1961. Their work resulted in the addition of about 60 species to the park list. Ecological studies carried on by Dr. Bettie Willard, now with the President's Council on Environmental Quality, throughout the park have furnished valuable environmental data as well as several additions to the list of species.

To name all the friends and colleagues who have given encouragement and assistance over the years would be impossible, but appreciation is expressed to all of them and also to members of the National Park Service and the Rocky Mountain Nature Association, especially Chief Park Naturalist Tom D. Thomas, who have wholeheartedly supported this project. In addition, appreciation goes to all the photographers who have generously allowed their photographs and transparencies to be used in this publication.

Ruth A. Nelson

Introduction

THE WILDFLOWERS of Rocky Mountain National Park are one of its main attractions. They paint its fields, meadows, hillsides, and rocky gorges in all the colors of the rainbow. There has been a constant demand for an illustrated guide to these flowers, and this publication has been prepared in response to that demand. It is the result of many years' study of the plants of the region. Emphasis has been put on the outstanding field characters of the plants described and on their habitats. Keys for identification and an illustrated glossary are included. The chapter on Mountain Plants at Home deals with the relationship between the plants and their severe mountain environment and their adaptations to that environment.

The keys have been made as practical and simple as possible. They have been previously published, tested, and revised, and the author feels that they will be useful to all persons who are seriously interested in the identification of the common wildflowers, whether or not they have had training in botany. In order to keep the keys from being long and unwieldy, some of the inconspicuous plants are not included. However, the names of all seed plants and ferns known to grow in the park are given in the text. Technical terms have been avoided as much as possible, but because it is impossible to differentiate between related plants by using only everyday English, some technical terms have been employed to assure accuracy. These are adequately explained by drawings and definitions in the glossary.

About 850 different kinds of plants are included. Specimens of most of these are in the herbarium of Rocky Mountain National Park. Many have been collected by the author. Only a few of the most conspicuous of the numerous kinds of grasses, sedges, and rushes are described, but the names of some common species known to occur within the park are listed. The region that has been intensively studied is that of the Rocky Mountain National Park and the immediate surroundings, but this book will be found useful above 7,000 feet throughout the mountains of northern Colorado and southern Wyoming.

A list of useful references to publications on various phases of plantlife in this region may be found in the back of the book.

Picking of wildflowers or the collection of any specimens of animals, trees, or minerals in all National Parks is prohibited without special permission of the park superintendent. Users of this book are urged to be mindful of this regulation. Study the plants where they grow, take home pictures of them, but leave them for others to enjoy.

Figure 1. Montane zone showing open forest of ponderosa pine with shrub and grass growth well developed between the trees.

Figure 2. A montane valley on the western slope near Shadow Mountain Lake. Here willows border the stream, sagebrush is well developed on sunny slopes, and lodgepole pine forests clothe the north-facing slopes and upper montane zone.

Figure 3. Lower montane zone showing sagebrush and Rocky Mountain juniper on south-facing slope, ponderosa pine above.

Figure 4. Montane streamside growth. Willows and narrowleaf poplar bordering the water. In similar situations, alder and birch might also be found —spruce in the next rank. Aspen along watercourse on upper slope.

Figure 5. Subalpine and alpine zones compared. Dense Engelmann spruce—subalpine fir forest at elevations between 10,000 and 11,500 feet—alpine grassland, tundra, in foreground and above. The dense forest extends higher on protected slopes than on exposed ones.

Scientific Names

Each distinct kind of plant has a technical name, which is written in the Latin language. Many, but not all, plants have common English names as well. The Latin names are usually descriptive of the plant to which they are applied, for example, *Chenopodium,* the goosefoot or lambsquarters. This Latin name is from two Greek words—*chen,* goose, and *podion,* little foot—and is descriptive of the shape of the leaves. It is the *generic* name and applies to all of the goosefoots as the name Smith applies to all members of the Smith family.

If we wish to speak of one particular kind of goosefoot, we apply a *specific* name which is a Latin descriptive adjective. The name *album,* meaning white, is given to the common lambsquarter, *Chenopodium album,* the white goosefoot, because of the white, powdery substance that covers the leaves of this plant. Sometimes, the botanist who named the plant wanted to honor one of his friends, so he named a plant for him. Fremont goosefoot, *Chenopodium fremontii,* is an example.

Botanically speaking, Latin is a universal language, and these Latin names have the advantage of being understood by all botanists no matter what their native language is. Common names are confusing, because there are not enough to go around, so in different parts of the country the same name is used for different plants. A person with a wide knowledge of plants can never be certain just what plant is being referred to when a common name is used. Consequently, students of plants prefer the scientific names.

Figure 6. A subalpine lake showing characteristic clumps of dwarfed spruce and low-growing willows.

Mountain Plants at Home

On all mountains of great height there exist climatic belts or zones. Zones of altitude on a mountain can be roughly compared to zones of latitude on the surface of the earth. A mountain situated at the Equator in a humid climate and reaching an altitude of 18,000 feet will carry approximately all the variations in environment that would be encountered on a trip from the Equator to the Arctic Circle. The altitude of timberline decreases with an increase in the latitude north. Timberline is at approximately 11,500 feet in north-central Colorado, although it may vary as much as 500 feet up or down due to local conditions, while in Montana it is at 9,000 feet and in Alberta at about 7,000 feet.

Each climatic area or zone supports a distinct association of plants and animals, which biologists call *life zones.* Of course, these associations merge into each other as their boundaries are approached. Some individuals have a much wider range than others, some range through several zones, and others are confined strictly to one. Those which are strictly limited in distribution become what are called *zone indicators.* By noting their distribution the ecologist can determine his elevation to within a few hundred feet. Zones are recognized for the entire continent and for animals as well as plants. Several different systems of zoning have been used by different authors, but the following arrangement seems the most practical for this region. Three vegetation zones or regions are represented in the Rocky Mountain National Park—the *montane,* 6,000 feet to 9,000 feet; the *subalpine,* from 9,000 feet to timberline (approximately 11,500 feet); and the *alpine,* above timberline.*

Environments are much influenced by local conditions of available moisture, prevailing winds, exposure, and topography. Timberline will be found much higher on the south exposure of a sheltered ravine than on a windswept ridge exposed to the north. For instance, as you travel westward toward the head of Hidden Valley on the Trail Ridge Road, the irregularity of timberline is quite noticeable. At the head of the valley, where the exposure is due east, it dips down in a distinct V formation. Apparently, this is caused by a large snowbank which remains in this location well into the summer and is so deep that it smothers seedling trees, allowing them no chance to get started. An additional factor here may be the cold air draining down the slope from the snowbank. On each side of this valley, trees extend higher than they do at its head, but on the right side where the exposure is toward the southeast they extend considerably higher than they do on the left side where it is toward the northeast. The same condition may be noted at the head of Fall River Valley.

*This zonation agrees with that given in *Plant Ecology,* by John L. Weaver and Frederic E. Clements, published by McGraw-Hill in 1929, and in *The Study of Plant Communities,* by Henry J. Oosting (Second Edition), published by W. H. Freeman & Co. in 1958.

Figure 7. On the heights, grassy tundra with many alpine flowers at about 12,000 feet, wind-shaped trees in middle distance and grove of short but erect Engelmann spruce in a protected hollow.

Figure 8. The forest frontier, where trees grow successively shorter until at timberline they become prostrate.

Figure 9. "Wind timber" or Krummholz—at timberline where the spruces become prostrate and severe winds shear and shape them.

Figure 10. Old limber pines on a stony, exposed ridge have finally succumbed. Younger ones are wind-whipped.

Climate and Vegetation Zones in Rocky Mountain National Park

All the lower slopes of the park are included in the montane zone (figs. 1-4 and 13). On the eastern slope is characteristically a region of open ponderosa pine forest, with the Douglas-fir intermixed. It includes moist and dry aspen groves, lodgepole, and Douglas-fir forest on north-facing slopes, open meadows, and barren, rocky ridges. In the lower montane, the ponderosa pine may be mixed with Rocky Mountain juniper (also called western red-cedar), and usually is so found on warm south-facing slopes (fig. 3). On the high, rocky points is some limber pine. Along the streams are found groves of the magnificent Colorado blue spruce associated with willows, alder, and water birch (fig. 4).

Many of the shrubs from the foothills are found here, where they reach their highest elevation. Antelope-brush with its small fragrant pale-yellow blossoms early in June, thimbleberry with large roselike white blooms (fig. 81) growing in the rockiest places, squawcurrant (fig. 80) almost everywhere with pungent, aromatic foliage, and little red currants—all are typical. There are also many characteristic flowering herbs here. The tall penstemon (fig. 138), wild geranium (fig. 96), kinnikinnic (fig. 111), shooting-star (fig. 119), and Porter aster are most numerous and reach their greatest development in this zone, but occasionally they will be found at both higher and lower altitudes. In the upper montane, ponderosa pine and Douglas-fir occur together on south-facing and on shaded north-facing slopes. Douglas-fir and lodgepole pine are often found together.

Figure 11. Plant succession on a shaded rock surface. The light and dark patches on the rock at the right and left sides are lichens. The dark cushions in center foreground are mosses. In the lower left corner is spike moss. In the crevice are pioneer ferns and alum root, at left foreground are grasses and other pioneer plants establishing themselves in the debris of rock particles, accumulated dead leaves, and pine needles.

Figure 13. Montane aspen grove. Notice the secondary succession taking place in the foreground, with the coniferous trees growing up among the aspens. Eventually the coniferous trees will grow larger than the aspens and shade them, so that the aspens will die.

Figure 12. Recently burned lodgepole pine forest, showing some new growth of herbs and deciduous shrubs. The charred logs lying on the ground are relics of an earlier fire. This shows the dense growth characteristic of lodgepole.

Figure 14. Mature subalpine Engelmann spruce—subalpine-fir forest, showing young trees replacing the fallen ones.

Figure 15. Banner trees near timberline showing effect of prevailing winds.

19

The scenery of the western slope has a different appearance. That side of the Continental Divide receives considerably more moisture in both snow and rain than the eastern side. This additional moisture has caused greater weathering of the rock, therefore the mountain slopes facing westward are less rugged and have deeper soils. Consequently, vegetative cover is more continuous, and growth more luxuriant. In the montane region, sagebrush covers the drier, south-facing slopes, and lodgepole pine is the dominant tree (see fig. 2).

Above the montane zone is the region of heavy Engelmann spruce-subalpine fir forest—the subalpine zone. This region receives the heaviest snowfall of any in the mountains. Because of the heavy forest, the snow remains late into the spring and sometimes well into the summer, insuring plentiful moisture throughout the short season. The abundance of moisture makes this zone the most luxuriant of all in vegetation (fig. 172). The forest is interrupted here and there by lakes and marshes and contains pure lodgepole stands on the places burned by forest fires and limber pine on the more exposed slopes.

Between approximately 10,500 and 11,500 feet is the transition from the subalpine to the alpine region. Timberline varies between these two extremes, according to the exposure and topography. This area contains luxuriant subalpine meadows (fig. 174), many lakes (fig. 6), considerable elfin or dwarf forest, and many exposed rocky ridges. Typical plants of the spruce forest are pipsissewa (fig. 110), star-flowered pyrola (fig. 108), one-sided pyrola, twinflower (fig. 148), and fairy slipper (fig. 34). Characteristic shrubs are mountain-ash (fig. 84) and the involucred honeysuckle or twinberry, both found along streams. Some subalpine flowers of the meadows and wet banks are pearly everlasting, fringed parnassia, ladies-tresses, brookcress, and rose crown (fig. 73a).

Timberline itself, with its gnarled and twisted trees, is one of the most interesting regions of the park (figs. 8 and 9). Here the wind and snow have combined to produce an elfin forest of fantastic appearance. Twisted trunks bearing branches only on their lee sides indicate the direction of the prevailing wind (fig. 15); trains of little trees, each one younger and shorter than the last, run out from the shelter of a big boulder or an old deformed tree (fig. 8). Often, gnarled old individuals stand isolated, but sometimes the trees are crowded, and their tops intermingle to such an extent as to be indistinguishable from one another. In many places, snowdrifts cover the dwarf trees, protecting them from the severe winds. Every little twig that sends a shoot above the snowline is promptly killed by the combined effect of the extreme cold and the desiccating wind. By this killing of the terminal shoot, the lateral buds below the snowline are stimulated to vigorous growth. This accounts in part for the denseness of these timberline thickets. In addition, the weight of the snow probably plays some part in their development along horizontal lines. Shelter from sudden mountain storms may be found under the dense, matted canopy of these treetops. Their trunks are sometimes as high as a man's head; in other places, they are prostrate on the ground, their branches forming low, rounded "windrows" a foot or two high, parallel to the direction of the prevailing winds and as neatly trimmed by the winds as though clipped by a hedge-trimmer's shears (fig. 9). Many an old dead snag, and often the windward side of a living tree, has been stripped of its bark and etched and carved by the tools of ice and sand carried by fierce alpine gales (fig. 10).

The trees which form the forest frontier in Rocky Mountain National Park are Engelmann spruce, subalpine fir, limber pine, and, rarely, lodgepole pine.

Clumps of dwarf willow and birch are seen high above timberline, dotting open slopes with their low, rounded masses.

Above timberline is the alpine zone (fig. 7). Here are grassland, meadows, and rockfields with the environment growing steadily more severe, culminating in the arctic conditions found on the highest peaks. Here are snowbanks the year around and freezing temperatures nearly every night. As the snow recedes, the flowers burst into bloom. The yellow snow buttercup (fig. 57), a large almost poppylike flower with much dissected leaves, and the white marsh-marigold (fig. 54) may be found breaking through the snow to bloom. The little bright blue alpine forget-me-not (fig. 131), the moss campion (fig. 52) with its cushion-like growth starred with pink blossoms, the Rydbergia (fig. 160) with its big golden head and its covering of shaggy white hair, the mountain dryad (fig. 83) with eight creamy petals and long plumed seeds, the tiny but gay rose-colored fairy primrose (fig. 115), the fragrant rock jasmine (fig. 118), and many more are all at home on these heights.

In June and July, the high rockfields, called fellfields, which appear at a little distance to be barren wastes, will be found on closer examination to be gay with the bright colors of the cushionlike plants which fill the spaces between the rocks (fig. 8). The effect is that of a brilliant crazy quilt spread out over the mountainside. One of the best examples of this may be seen in June on the north slope of Twin Sisters just before the summit is reached. A little later these plants are in their prime on Fall River Pass, Trail Ridge, Flattop Mountain, Longs Peak, and the other high peaks. Although tiny, almost all these plants are perenial and live for many years.

Adaptation to Environment

The mountain climate is severe because of the strong winds, dry atmosphere, low soil moisture in many places, and the exceptionally strong sunlight. Consequently, many mountain plants have developed special provisions which protect them from excessive evaporation.

The little alpine forget-me-not is covered by a cloak of soft silky hairs which forms an air space around it, thus retarding evaporation from the surface of the leaves. Many other plants are covered with hairs or wool; for instance, the scorpion weed, the miners candle (fig. 133), the Rydbergia, and the sulphur flower. In other plants, this protection is obtained by the presence of a hard outer cuticle over the epidermis of the leaf. On certain leaves, there is a layer of wax in addition to the cuticle. Cuticle and waxy layer are both present on the leaves of many evergreens that grow in a temperate climate. During the winter, the plant must not lose the moisture that is in its cells because little more will be available until spring. Many plants, especially those with large soft leaves, shed their leaves at the approach of the dry season. The plants (kinnikinnic, fig. 111, and mountain lover) that keep their leaves throughout the winter, or dry season, have tough, thick leaves with a hard surface, and the deep-set stomata are well protected. In the case of the pine family, the danger from too much evaporation is further lessened by the reduction in area of leaf surface. In some members, the stomata are set in grooves and the needles covered with a waxy coating. This wax is what gives the blue spruce its characteristic color. It is often noticeable on other conifers, giving them a bluish or silvery tinge.

Many of the grasses and some other plants have the margins of the leaves in-rolled. This device reduces the leaf surface exposed to the dry air and is a very effective means of preventing loss of moisture. Storage of water for future use in thick leaves and stems is another form of adaptation, commoner with plants of desert regions than with mountain plants, but noticeable in the stonecrops and some of the saxifrages. In these cases, the leaves are usually smooth, though not always so, and are often covered with a *glaucous bloom* (the waxy covering already described). The thickening of the leaf also results in a decreased surface area in relation to the volume, an added advantage.

Study of Plant Succession

Succession of plantlife from the first inhabitant of the bare rock to the climax type of vegetation for the region follows a definite course. In a mountainous region, such as Rocky Mountain National Park, succession is particularly interesting and easy to study because all stages may usually be found within a very short distance. On dry rocks, it begins with the crustose lichens (fig. 11). These occur in different shades of gray and green, yellow, and bright orange. All lichens become more brightly colored as soon as wet. These crustose lichens are the earliest pioneers, sticking tightly to the rocks and often spreading over them in circular patterns. They live, die, and are succeeded by their descendants for many years until a thin layer of humus has collected which will hold a little moisture and collect a little dust. Soil begins to form and then come the foliose or leafy lichens which make the layer a little thicker, so that mosses and a few grasses can get a foothold. Following these come some or all of the following pioneer plants: cinquefoil, grouseberry, kinnikinnic, golden banner, and wild pink geranium. In the crevices of the rocks, alumroot and seedlings of pine or some of the pioneer shrubs, such as juniper, jamesia, and thimbleberry, will begin to grow. Their leaves drop down and decay; gradually, the crevice is filled with soil. Underneath all this the rock is slowly crumbling, a process due partly to the slightly acid action of the ground water and the root excretions, but mostly to alternating heat and cold and to frost action. By this time, the seeds of other trees and shrubs will have lodged here and be able to germinate and grow in the protection afforded by this pioneer nursery. Finally, after thousands of years, in the montane zone are open grassy slopes dotted with ponderosa pines and Douglas-firs, and in the subalpine zone, close forests of spruce and fir.

Succession will occur much faster on wet rocks and along streambanks. Water-loving plants rather than drought-resisting ones will occupy the area. Much more growth will take place each season so that humus and soil will accumulate more rapidly. In this case, algae and mosses are the pioneers, followed by swamp, sedges, and grasses, next by willows and birches, and by aspens or lodgepole pines, and these eventually, in the subalpine, by spruce forest (fig. 14).

Where man or fire interferes, the succession progresses somewhat differently. In such cases, usually some soil is left, and a few living plants which reseed the area. After a forest fire in an open ponderosa pine forest, this same forest usually reestablishes itself without any intervening forest of a different kind, but when fire wipes out a close stand of mixed pine and Douglas-fir or of Engelmann spruce, a different story follows. After the fire, elder, aspen, fireweed, lupine, golden banner, grouseberry, and kinnikinnic begin to cover the ground. Normally, the following year, lodgepole seedlings come up in abundance, with willows and aspens in the areas of greatest moisture. The young lodgepoles and aspens require abundant sun, and a place where fire has made a clean sweep affords them an ideal home.

Under favorable conditions, as many as 50 lodgepole seedlings to a square yard will come up (fig. 12). As they grow taller, of course, they crowd each other, and some die because of competition for light and moisture. This closeness of habit results in dense stands found in many places in the park. Three lodgepole forests of different ages, each the result of a fire, may be seen from a point on the

Bear Lake Road about 5 miles from the Beaver Meadows Entrance Station. Just across the stream on the lower level is the youngest, a very dense stand where a fire occurred in June 1946. The seedlings came up that same summer, and in 1969 the trees averaged 10 feet in height. To the right and left is a dense stand of older, taller trees; above and behind the central group and along the roadbank are larger trees of an even older generation. Much of that region has been burned several times. A lodgepole forest constitutes a much greater fire hazard than any other forest because of the closeness of the trees, their pitch-iness, and comparative dryness. Fires in lodgepole forests are sometimes caused by lightning but usually by the carelessness of man.

The lodgepole and aspen forests are also merely a phase, and, if the succession is not interrupted by fire or logging, will give way eventually to other species. Given a chance to reach an age of 70 to 100 years, lodgepole forests will be in-vaded by Engelmann spruce, subalpine fir, or Douglas-fir. This is beginning to happen in the forest on Twin Sisters Mountain and on Trail Ridge. A few spruces may now be seen here and there among the lodgepoles. Seedling spruces do not usually thrive in sunlight and must get their start where they have some protection.

In the Bear Lake region after the fire of 1900, many dead trees were left standing, and many more were strewn on the ground, so that the ground itself was quite shaded. In addition, it is probable that this ground is a little too moist for the best development of lodgepole. Here many Engelmann spruce seedlings and some subalpine firs have started to grow and have managed to survive, along with the lodgepoles which occupy the sunnier places. In 40 or 50 years, the hills around Bear Lake and along Mill Creek may be covered with a mixed forest of lodgepole, Engelmann spruce, and subalpine fir. The former will even-tually be crowded out by the others, and the forest will then be what is termed the *climax* forest for this region—Engelmann spruce mixed with subalpine fir (fig. 14) and will perpetuate itself indefinitely unless destroyed by some outside agency.

Plants resemble people in some of their habits. Some are extremely aggres-sive; others are shy and retiring. The aggressive ones are often the ones that man calls weeds. They are the ones that will stand being trampled upon, that thrive on freshly turned ground, or for some reason flourish around buildings and along roadways. Man's activities of plowing, building, and roadmaking dis-turb the native plants of retiring habit, and, by their disappearance, the ground is left open for the aggressive invaders. Many of these are not natives, but their seed is carried in various ways, sometimes in hay, in the fur of animals, or in the seed that the farmer buys. Years ago the common dandelion did not exist in Estes Park, but now not only the dandelion and the Russian-thistle but many more weeds have been introduced from all over this country and Europe.

Some of the natives are aggressive also. Fields that have at one time been plowed and then abandoned can be distinguished for many years by the vegeta-tion on them, entirely different from that on the natural grassland. The native species commonest on these fields are stickseed, fringed mountain-sage, gum-weed, and tansy aster. Grama grass, one of the characteristic native grasses of open fields and slopes, does not begin to reestablish itself for 5 or 6 years after the original grassland vegetation has been disturbed.

A KEY FOR THE IDENTIFICATION OF THE COMMON AND CONSPICUOUS PLANTS OF ROCKY MOUNTAIN NATIONAL PARK

A. Woody Plants, Trees, Shrubs, or Vines

X. Plants parasitic, brownish or yellowish, never green in any part....................**Mistletoe** (p. 54)

XX. Plants not parasitic, always with green leaves.

  Y. Leaves evergreen, needlelike, or if broad, usually thick and shiny.

    a. Leaves needlelike, scalelike, or awlshaped.......................**Pine family** (p. 38)

    aa. Leaves neither needlelike nor scalelike, usually flat, low shrubs.

      b. Leaves definitely opposite.

        c. Flowers axillary, greenish, or maroon, inconspicuous;

          leaves glossy.........................**Mountain lover** (p. 89)

        cc. Flowers in terminal umbels or corymbs, rose-red;

          leaves dull...............................**Bog laurel** (p. 98)

      bb. Leaves alternate.

        c. Leaves compound, leaflets with spine-tipped teeth, hollylike.........**Creeping hollygrape** (p. 70)

        cc. Leaves simple with smooth edges, no spine-tipped teeth present

          d. Leaves 1 inch long or less, plant trailing...............**Kinnikinnic** (p. 98)

          dd. Leaves more than 1 inch long, often sticky;

            plant not trailing.........................**Mountain balm** (p. 89)

  YY. Leaves not evergreen, usually not both thick and shiny.

    a. Trees.

      b. Bark on young trees smooth and whitish or greenish; if gray, rough

        and furrowed; buds not stalked.

        c. Leaves roundish; tree very common, usually found in groves..........**Quaking aspen** (p. 52)

        cc. Leaves longer than broad; not common.

          d. Leaves broad at base and tapering to apex, pale

            underneath................................**Balsam poplar** (p. 51)

          dd. Leaves narrower and tapering to both ends, green

            underneath.......................**Narrowleaf cottonwood** (p. 51) bb. Bark gray or yellowish-gray, smooth; leaves with toothed margins, buds stalked . . . . **Thinleaf alder** (p. 54)

aa. Shrubs or trailing plants.

  b. Leaves definitely opposite.

    c. Plant climbing or trailing on the ground. . . . . **Clematis** (p. 67)

    cc. Plant erect.

      d. Leaves compound; flowers white, in a cluster . . . . **Redberried elder** (p. 119)

      dd. Leaves not compound; flowers various.

        e. Leaves lobed and sharply toothed.

          f. Plants often growing in dense clumps; fruit two-winged . . . . **Rocky Mountain maple** (p. 89)

          ff. Plants not growing in dense clumps; fruit a red berry . . . . **High bush cranberry** (p. 119)

        ee. Leaves not markedly lobed nor sharply toothed.

          f. Flowers few.

            g. Flowers yellow, in pairs, ripening into black, shiny berries; leaves over
              2 inches long . . . . **Twinberry** (p. 119)

            gg. Flowers pinkish, ripening into white berries; leaves less than
              2 inches long . . . . **Snowberry** (p. 119)

          ff. Flowers many, in clusters, white.

            g. Bark red or reddish-brown, smooth. . . . . **Red-osier dogwood** (p. 96)

            gg. Bark gray, shreddy . . . . **Jamesia** (p. 78)

  bb. Leaves alternate.

    c. Buds enclosed in one caplike scale, plants may be very low creeping shrubs
      to almost tree size. . . . . **Willow** (p. 52)

    cc. Buds enclosed in several overlapping scales.

      d. Plant thorny or spiny.

        e. Leaves compound.

          f. Leaflets three to five; flowers white . . . . **Wild red raspberry** (p. 82)

          ff. Leaflets five to seven; flowers pink or rose. **Wild rose** (p. 82)

        ee. Leaves not compound.

          f. Leaves entire or nearly so; plant very low, flowers white. . . . . **Fendler buckthorn** (p.89)

          ff. Leaves lobed or toothed or both.

            g. Spines stout, 1 to 2 inches long; flowers white. . . . . **Fireberry hawthorn** (p. 82)

            gg. Spines slender, not over one-half inch long; flowers pinkish or greenish.

h. Flowers tubular; berries one to four, smooth..........**Mountain gooseberry** (p. 77)

hh. Flowers saucer or bowl-shaped, berries several, bristly..........**Prickly currant** (p. 77)

dd. Plant not thorny nor spiny.

  e. Leaves compound.

    f. Leaflets three, sometimes lobed; flowers inconspicuous..........**Three-leaf sumac** (p. 88)

    ff. Leaflets more than three.

      g. Leaflets five to seven, entire; flowers yellow..........**Shrubby cinquefoil** (p. 81)

      gg. Leaflets 11 to 15, serrate; flowers in large clusters, white..........**Greenes mountain-ash** (p. 84)

  ee. Leaves not compound.

    f. Leaves lobed or deeply toothed.

      g. Leaves three-toothed at apex, not over 1½ inches long, somewhat wedge-shaped.

        h. Bush silver-gray, aromatic..........**Sagebrush** (p. 139)

        hh. Bush neither silver-gray nor aromatic..........'..**Antelope-brush** (p. 82)

      gg. Leaves three- to seven-lobed, oval, roundish or heart-shaped in outline.

        h. Flowers white, not tubular nor bell-shaped.

          i. Flowers 1 to 2 inches across..........**Rocky Mountain thimbleberry** (p. 82)

          ii. Flowers small, in clusters.

            j. Clusters flat or rounded on top..........**Mountain ninebark** (p. 82)

            jj. Clusters pyramidal..........**Mountain spray** (p. 81)

        hh. Flowers pink, greenish, or yellowish, tubular or bell-shaped.

          i. Leaves 1½ to 2 inches broad, fruit black..........**Colorado currant** (p. 78)

          ii. Leaves less than 1½ inches broad, fruit red..........**Squaw currant** (p. 77)

    ff. Leaves never lobed, entire or merely slightly toothed.

      g. Plants low, not over 1 foot high.

        h. Flowers in catkins, buds with only one, caplike scale..........**Willow** (p. 52)

        hh. Flowers not in catkins, buds with overlapping scales.

          i. Flowers urn-shaped, pinkish or white; fruit a juicy berry.

27

    j. Leaves less than ½-inch long,
        berries red, branches green. . . . . **Grouseberry** (p. 98)
    jj. Leaves mostly over ½-inch long,
        berry black or bluish, branches mostly brown . . . . **Myrtleleaf blueberry** (p. 98)
  ii. Flower saucer-shaped, eight-petaled; plant dwarf
        and matted . . . . **Mountain dryad** (p. 79)
gg. Plants taller.
  h. Plants growing in wet places; flowers in catkins.
    i. Leaves serrate.
      j. Bark reddish-brown and shiny; leaves pointed. . . . . **Water birch** (p. 54)
      jj. Bark black; twigs rough with whitish glands;
          leaves rounded. **Bog birch** (p. 54)
    ii. Leaves usually entire; bark smooth, gray, green,
        yellow, or reddish. . . . . **Willow** (p. 53)
  hh. Plants not confined to wet places; flowers not in catkins.
    i. New twigs and buds rust color; under side
        of leaves silvery. **Bitter buffaloberry** (p. 92)
    ii. New twigs and buds not rust color;
        leaves green underneath.
      j. Leaves oval or roundish. . . . . **Serviceberry** (p. 82)
      jj. Leaves at least half again as long as broad,
          usually tapering at both ends
        k. Flowers white, in a raceme, fruit black. . . . . **Chokecherry** (p. 84)
        kk. Flowers white, in an umbel, fruit red. . . . . **Birdcherry** (p. 84)

AA. Nonwoody Plants

X. Plants never bearing true flowers (Pteridophytes, i. e., "fern plants").
  Y. Plants with broad leaves usually much dissected..**Fern family** (p. 34)
  YY. Plants with needlelike, awllike, or toothlike leaves, or apparently none.
    a. Plants with hollow, jointed green stems; no evident leaves..............**Horsetail family** (p. 37)
    aa. Plants with solid and continuous stems; awllike leaves present.......**Clubmoss family** (p. 38)
XX. Plants bearing true flowers (Spermatophytes, i e., "seed plants").
  Y. Plants aquatic, growing partly or entirely submersed in water, bearing conspicuous flowers or fruits.
    a. Leaves simple and entire.
      b. Leaves not linear.
        c. Leaves 4 to 12 inches long, floating; flowers 2 to 5 inches across, yellow.......**Yellow pondlily** (p. 61)
        cc. Leaves 2 to 6 inches long; flowers not yellow.
          d. Leaves oval or lanceolate, floating; flowers bright pink.............**Water buckwheat** (p. 57)
          dd. Leaves erect, arrowhead shaped; flowers small, white..................**Arrowhead** (p. 39)
      bb. Leaves linear, floating; fruit a burlike cluster of achenes................**Bur-reed** (p. 39)
    aa. Leaves compound or finely dissected; flowers white or yellow, not in spikes....**Buttercup family** (p. 63)
  YY. Plants terrestrial, never floating but sometimes growing on very wet ground.
    a. Plants without green foliage, parasites or saprophytes.
      b. Parasites growing on branches of coniferous trees.......................**Mistletoe family** (p. 54)
      bb. Parasites or saprophytes growing on the ground, on roots or dead wood.
        c. Plant hairy.
          d. Plant 10 to 60 inches high; flowers nodding.........................**Pinedrops** (p. 99)
          dd. Plant 6 inches high or less; flowers erect.........................**Broomrape** (p. 117)
        cc. Plant smooth...**Coralroot** (p. 51)
    aa. Plants with green foliage.
      b. Plants with parallel-veined leaves; flower parts if brightly colored in three's or sixes (Monocotyledons).
        c. Plants 3 to 6 feet high; flowers small, in dense brown spikes...............**Cattail** (p. 39)
        cc. Plants usually less than 3 feet high.
          d. Plants grasslike or rushlike; flowers numerous and inconspicuous.
            e. Stems round or flattened.
              f. Stems jointed; leaf blades flat......................................**Grass family** (p. 40)
              ff. Stems not jointed; leaf blades round or flat.........................**Rush family** (p. 44)

29

ee. Stems usually three-angled . . . . **Sedge family** (p. 43)

dd. Plants not grasslike or rushlike, or if so, with colored flowers.

e. Flowers regular, with six perianth segments and three or six stamens.

f. Flowers usually blue; leaves two-ranked; ovary inferior . . . . **Iris family** (p. 49)

ff. Flowers not blue; leaves not two-ranked; ovary superior . . . . **Lily family** (p. 46)

ee. Flowers irregular, the lower petal usually sac-shaped or spurred . . . . **Orchid family** (p. 49)

bb. Plants with netted-veined leaves; flower parts usually in fours or fives (Dictyledons).

c. Flowers clustered in dense heads, the head surrounded by bracts and often resembling a single flower . . . . **Composite family** (p. 120)

cc. Flowers not in a dense head surrounded by bracts (except in clover).

d. Leaves opposite.

e. Plants with milky juice.

f. Leaves petioled, more than 1 inch long . . . . **Indian-hemp** (p. 103)

ff. Leaves and bracts sessile, 1 inch or less long, bracts opposite . . . . **Spurge** (p. 88)

ee. Plants without milky juice.

f. Corolla of separate petals or absent.

g. Stems swollen at the joints; flowers never yellow.

h. Flowers in small clusters, each subtended by an involucre; fruit one-seeded . . . . **Wild four-o'clock** (p. 58)

hh. Flowers never subtended by an involucre.

i. Fruit many-seeded, leaves without stipules . . . . **Pink family** (p. 60)

ii. Fruit one-seeded, leaves with scarious stipules . . . . **Rocky Mountain nailwort** (p. 61)

gg. Stems not swollen at the joints; petals thin.

h. Flowers yellow; leaves with translucent dots . . . . **St. Johnswort** (p. 91)

hh. Flowers pink or white with pink veins, leaves not dotted . . . . **Purslane family** (p. 58)

ff. Corolla of united petals.

g. Stem square, distinctly four-angled.

h. Leaves more than two at each node . . . . **Bedstraw** (p. 119)

hh. Leaves two at each node.

i. Plant branched from the base and spreading on the ground . . . . **Vervain** (p. 109)

ii. Plant usually erect, usually aromatic. . . . . **Mint family** (p. 109)

gg. Stem usually round, not four-angled.

h. Plant a trailing vine with paired, pink blossoms. . . . . **Twinflower** (p. 119)

hh. Plants not trailing vines with paired blossoms.

i. Seed pod one-seeded and inferior. **Valerian** (p. 120)

ii. Seed pod several seeded and superior.

j. Corolla regular.

k. Plant a diminutive shrub of boggy ground

at high altitudes. . . . . **Bog laurel** (p. 98)

kk. Plants not shrubs.

l. Plant 1 to 3 inches high, forming

dense mats in alpine zone;

flowers pale blue or white. . . . . **Tufted phlox** (p. 105)

ll. Plants usually taller; not

matted, flowers mostly bright

or dark blue. . . . . **Gentian family** (p. 101)

jj. Corolla irregular. . . . . **Figwort family** (p. 110)

dd. Leaves alternate or all basal.

e. Leaves with papery sheathing bases, or all basal and then the

numerous small yellow flowers in umbels. . . . . **Buckwheat family** (p. 54)

ee. Leaves without papery sheathing bases and flowers not as above.

f. Petals separate.

g. Flowers very small, in umbels; leaves compound.

h. Stems hollow; petioles enlarged and sheathing the stem. . . . . **Parsnip family** (p. 95)

hh. Stems not hollow; petioles not enlarged and not

sheathing the stem. . . . . **Wild-sarsaparilla** (p. 95)

gg. Flowers not usually in umbels; stems not hollow.

h. Leaves composed of five to seven hollylike leaflets. . . . . **Creeping hollygrape** (p. 70)

hh. Leaves not composed of hollylike leaflets.

i. Stamens many, at least more than 10.

j. Filaments united into a column. . . . . **Mallow family** (p. 89)

jj. Filaments, not united.

k. Sepals, not united.
  l. Foliage glaucous with many straw-
    colored prickles. . . . . **Pricklypoppy** (p. 70)
  ll. Foliage not glaucous, without
    prickles. . . . . **Buttercup family** (p. 63)
kk. Sepals united, at least at base.
  l. Calyx saucerlike or cup-shaped. **Rose family** (p. 78)
  ll. Calyx enclosing the inferior ovary
    and forming a cylindrical or
    ovoid seedpod.
    m. Stems very rough, leaves evident. . . . . **Loasa family** (p. 91)
    mm. Stems thick, dull green, covered
      with tufts of spines, no leaves
      evident. . . . . **Cactus family** (p. 92)
ii. Stamens not more than 10.
  j. Stamens twice as many as the pistils.
    k. Plants very smooth, leaves fleshy. . . . . **Stonecrop family** (p. 74)
    kk. Plants more or less hairy, leaves
      not fleshy. . . . . **Geranium family** (p. 86)
  jj. Stamens usually four to 10 (may be many in
    Purslane and Rose families).
    k. Petals five (many in bitterroot), stamens
      usually five or 10.
      l. Flowers regular.
        m. Petals blue. . . . . **Blue flax** (p. 88)
        mm. Petals not blue.
          n. Leaves neither compound
            nor deeply cut.
            o. Plants smooth, never
              hairy nor sticky.
              p. Leaves firm,
                evergreen. . . . . **Pyrola** (p. 96)

pp. Leaves soft, succulent .... **Purslane family** (p. 58)

oo. Plants usually some- what hairy or sticky, except in *Parnassia* .... **Saxifrage family** (p. 74)

nn. Leaves compound or deeply cut; stamens usually many .... **Rose family** (p. 78)

ll. Flowers irregular.

  m. Leaves simple .... **Violet family** (p. 91)

  mm. Leaves compound .... **Pea family** (p. 84)

kk. Petals four, stamens six or eight.

  l. Sepals two, flowers irregular, yellow .... **Golden smoke** (p. 70)

  ll. Sepals four, flowers regular.

    m. Ovary superior.

      n. Leaves three-foliolate, pod stalked .... **Rocky Mountain beeplant** (p. 72)

      nn. Leaves not three-foliolate, pod not stalked .... **Mustard family** (p. 70)

    mm. Ovary inferior, stamens eight .... **Evening-primrose family** (p. 92)

ff. Petals united.

g. Corolla regular.

  h. Corolla urn-shaped; fruit a berry .... **Heath family** (p. 96)

  hh. Corolla bell-shaped, funnel or salver-form.

    i. Fruit consisting of four nutlets, sometimes prickly .... **Borage family** (p. 106)

    ii. Fruit consisting of a many-seeded pod.

      j. Stamens conspicuously protruding .... **Waterleaf family** (p. 106)

      jj. Stamens not protruding

        k. Calyx free from the superior ovary.

          l. Leaves simple and basal (except in loosestrife) .... **Primrose family** (p. 99)

          ll. Leaves not all basal, often compound or divided .... **Phlox family** (p. 103)

        kk. Calyx closely attached to the inferior ovary .... **Bellflower family** (p. 120)

gg. Corolla irregular .... **Figwort family** (p. 110)

33

Families of Plants

ADDERSTONGUE FAMILY *(OPHIOGLOSSACEAE)*

Grapeferns, *Botrychium lunaria, Botrychium lanceolatum,* and *Botrychium matricariaefolium* are found in the lower subalpine on dry, grassy banks. These are small inconspicuous plants, having the fertile and sterile fronds born on the same stalk. The fertile fronds are longer than the sterile ones and appear as an erect bunch of very small grapes. Each plant has only one sterile frond.

FERN FAMILY *(POLYPODIACEAE)*

FERNS ARE NOT VERY NUMEROUS in this region because of the dry climate and, with the exception of two or three species, are rarely seen. They are most commonly found in either wet or dry rocky situations in crevices, under cliffs or against rocks and occur most frequently in subalpine regions, although a few species are occasionally seen at lower or higher altitudes. Ferns are a lower order of plant life than the flowering plants and do not produce seeds. Instead, they reproduce by minute bodies called *spores* which are borne in little cases called *sporangia*. These *sporangia* (singular *sporangium*) occur in small clusters called "fruit dots" or *sori* (singular *sorus*), on the backs of the fronds. In some species, the sorus is covered with a thin scalelike structure called the *indusium*.

A. Frond very little dissected, apparently more grasslike than fernlike.......
                                                 Grass-leaved fern (p. 37)
AA. Frond dissected.
  B. Fronds of one kind, all alike.
    a. Fronds once pinnate, plants rare, mostly evergreen.
      b. Pinnae thin and fragile, narrowed at the base and attached at
        a point..................**Maidenhair spleenwort** (p. 37)
      bb. Pinnae tough, evergreen, attached by their whole width.
        c. Frond 3 to 6 inches long; sori with no indusium; growing
          mostly in rock crevices........**Western polypody** (p. 35)
        cc. Fronds usually 10 inches long or longer; indusium kidney
          shaped, conspicuous; plants very rare..................
                         Mountain holly fern (p. 35)
  aa. Fronds more than once pinnate, not evergreen.
    b. Fronds long and tapering.
      c. Fronds 10 inches to 3 feet long.
        d. Sori long or crescent-shaped; indusium conspicuous....
                       Common lady fern (p. 35)
        dd. Sori round.
          e. Indusium evident.......**Mountain wood fern** (p. 37)
          ee. Indusium not evident.......**Alpine lady fern** (p. 35)
      cc. Fronds 3 to 8 inches long.
        d. Plants tufted, old brown leaf bases persistent.
          e. Rachis and underside of fronds hairy; divisions long-
           triangular.......**Rocky Mountain woodsia** (p. 37)
          ee. Rachis and underside of fronds mostly smooth; divi-
           sions short-triangular.....**Oregon woodsia** (p. 37)
        dd. Plants not tufted; old leaf bases not present..........
                           Brittle fern (p. 35)

        bb. Fronds nearly as broad as long; often three-parted.
            c. Fronds soft and thin, a foot high or less . . . **Oak fern** (p. 37)
            cc. Fronds firm and leathery, 1 to 4 feet high. . . . .
                                        Western bracken (p. 35)
    BB. Fronds of two kinds, the fertile ones taller.
        a. Stipes distinct, slender, tufted. . . . . **Parsley fern** (p. 35)
        aa. Stipes stout, fertile and sterile fronds on one stalk. . **Grape ferns** in
                                        Adderstongue family (p. 34)

Brittle fern, *Cystopteris fragilis.*—A small fern with very fragile fronds, as its scientific name implies. The frond is tapering, usually twice-pinnate, and rarely over 8 inches in length. This is the commonest, widely distributed fern in the park as well as one of the most widely distributed in the world. It will be found in moist places on banks and cliffs, under ledges, and in rock crevices at all altitudes. It has been found on the summit of both Specimen Mountain and Trail Ridge above 12,000 feet. The very rare *Cystopteris montana* has been found on the western slope.

Western bracken, *Pteridium aquilinum* var. *pubescens.*—A stout plant, 1 to 4 feet high, with a tough, leathery frond, which has usually three to seven triangular divisions. It is also one of the most widely distributed ferns in the world, but in the park it is confined to the montane zone. It may be found in either sun or shade, usually in sandy or rocky soil, and is abundant on the Fern Lake Trail below the Pool. The young shoots of this plant were used by some of the western Indians for food.

Alpine lady fern, *Athyrium americanum* var. *alpestre* (fig. 16). — A rather large fern, with very delicate and lacy, tapering light-green fronds 10 inches to 3 feet long, found in the upper subalpine and alpine zones often in full sun and usually in very wet places. It is conspicuous along streams and in meadows between Dream and Emerald Lakes and has been found at Lake of Glass and in Wild Basin. It also grows in the Sierra Nevada, in Quebec, Alaska, and the mountains of Europe and Asia. The **common lady fern,** *Athyrium filix-femina,* with large dark green tapering fronds and elongated sori, is found occasionally in wet places of the lower subalpine and montane zones.

Western polypody, *Polypodium vulgare (Plypodium hesperium),* with once-pinnate fronds and large yellowish sori, is occasionally found in rock crevices throughout this region, but is nowhere common.

Mountain hollyfern, *Polystichum lonchitis,* is a rare evergreen fern of the subalpine, with long narrow, once-pinnate fronds. The pinnae are serrate and have lobes on the lower margins next the rachis. It resembles the **eastern Christmas fern,** *Polystichum acrostichoides.*

Parsley fern, or **American rockbrake,** *Cryptogramma crispa* ssp. *acrostichoides* (fig. 17), is the only member of this family within the park having two kinds of fronds. The short parsley-like fronds carry on the functions of leaves, and the taller, narrower fronds are specialized for spore bearing. These fronds are more yellowish in color, each segment is slightly podlike and contains many spores. This is a rock-crevice fern of the subalpine region and is often found in full sun. It is mainly confined to western North America and is abundant in the Sierra Nevada as well as in the Rocky Mountains.

Figure 17. **Parsley fern.**

Figure 16. **Alpine lady fern.**

Figure 18. **Lodgepole pine, flowers and young cones.**

Figure 19. **Lodgepole branches with cones of several yea**

Figure 20. **Subalpine fir, tip of tree with cones.**

Figure 21. **Blue spruce branches with young cones.**

The **woodsias** are small tufted ferns of dry, often exposed rocky situations. The stipes of last year's fronds are usually present and of a reddish-brown color. There are two species similar in appearance and difficult to distinguish. The **Oregon woodsia,** *Woodsia oregana,* has the back of the frond smooth and is most commonly found in the montane region, especially under shelving rocks, while the **Rocky Mountain woodsia,** *Woodsia scopulina,* has white jointed hairs on the back of the frond and is more commonly found in the subalpine and alpine zones. Both are exclusively North American ferns and mainly western in distribution.

Other ferns that may be found are: **oak fern,** *Gymnocarpium dryopteris,* a delicate fern of shady places, with triangular, three-parted fronds; **mountain wood fern,** *Dryopteris assimilis,* and **male fern,** *Dryopteris filix-mas,* found in the subalpine zone: **maidenhair spleenwort,** *Asplenium trichomanes,* a fern of moist rock crevices, very rare in this region; **Fendler lipfern,** *Cheilanthes fendleri,* grows on rocky hillsides near Estes Park; and the **zigzag cloak fern,** *Notholaena fendleri,* grows on dry cliffs of foothill canyons east of the park. The **grass-leaved fern,** *Asplenium septentrionale,* grows in tufts in dry rock crevices. It is a curious plant appearing to the casual observer more like a grass than a fern. It may be recognized by the black, shiny base of the rachis and by the rusty-colored sori along the margins at the tips of the narrow fronds.

HORSETAIL FAMILY *(EQUISETACEAE)*

The **horsetails** and **scouring-rushes** are plants with hollow, jointed green stems and apparently no leaves. The leaves are reduced to very small toothlike scales around the joints of the stem and to scales which make up a conelike fruiting structure called a *strobilus* (plural *strobili*). These strobili grow on the tips of the stems. The stems contain chlorophyll, the green substance which, in the presence of sunlight, enables plant tissues to manufacture food, so that these stems perform the function of leaves. They also contain minute particles of silica which give them their scouring quality. These plants are closely related to the ferns and reproduce by means of spores which are borne in spore cases on the scales of the strobili.

Horsetail, *Equisetum arvense.*—A plant 4 to 18 inches high, frequently found in the park. It has two kinds of stems, the fertile unbranched stems, pale brownish in color, bearing the strobili, and sterile green stems with whorls of slender branches, which give it its horsetail-like appearance. The fertile stems disappear early in the season, so that often only the sterile ones are found. This plant is widely distributed throughout this country and Europe; it is often found along railroad embankments. In the park, it occurs along roads and trails on moist soil.

Smooth horsetail, *Equisetum laevigatum.*—This plant is much less common than the former and much larger. The stem may be 1 to 3 feet high and ½-inch in diameter and is usually unbranched. The stems are annual. Both the fertile and sterile ones are green. It is found on sandy soil. *Equisetum laevigatum* is similar, but its stems are evergreen. Another evergreen species reported for this area is *Equisetum hyemale.*

QUILLWORT FAMILY *(ISOËTACEAE)*

Quillworts are found in shallow waters of ponds and lakes where muck has accumulated. They appear like small stiff tufts of submerged grass, but they do not have flowers. The leaves have bulb-like bases where the spores are born. Unlike grasses, their leaves radiate in all directions. *Isoëtes bolanderi* has been collected from subalpine lakes throughout the park, and *Isoëtes occidentalis* is found at Grand Lake.

CLUBMOSS FAMILY *(LYCOPODIACEAE)*

Groundpine, *Lycopodium annotinum.*—Occasionally found in moist situations in the subalpine zone. A creeping evergreen plant, with flattened, awl-shaped leaves arranged in several ranks, and twice-forking branches. The rare **fir clubmoss,** *Lycopodium selago,* smaller than the groundpine, has also been found.

SPIKEMOSS FAMILY *(SELAGINELLACEAE)*

Spikemosses, or **"little clubmosses,"** are rarely noticed because of their small size, but they play an important part in the building up of fertile soil on dry barren ground and sometimes on rock surfaces. Where other vegetation is scanty, these little plants fill in many vacancies with mats of their creeping stems. Ordinarily gray, they become beautifully green in wet weather. The so-called "resurrection plant" of Mexico belongs to this family. **Rock spikemoss,** *Selaginella densa,* is the commonest species here, growing at all elevations. Tiny orange bodies in the axils of the leaves contain the *megaspores* from which new plants will grow. *Selaginella mutica,* a slenderer plant; **Underwoods spikemoss,** *Selaginella underwoodii,* which forms a network of slender stems; and *Selaginella scopulorum* are also found.

PINE FAMILY *(PINACEAE)*

The nine species of coniferous trees included in the following key occur in the park*:

Leaves needlelike, 1 inch long or longer; seeds in cones.
  Leaves occurring in bundles of two to five, three-cornered or crescent-shaped in cross section.
    Leaves two in each bundle; cones remaining on the trees for many years . . . . **Lodgepole pine** (figs. 18 and 19)
                  Pinus contorta var. *latifolia*
    Leaves three, two, or five in bundle, cones falling when mature.
      Leaves three (or two) in each bundle; bark of mature trees reddish-yellow . . . . **Ponderosa pine** (fig. 1)
                  Pinus ponderosa
      Leaves five in each bundle; bark of mature trees grayish-black . . . . **Limber pine** (fig. 10)
                  Pinus flexilis

*For detailed descriptions of these trees, see Rocky Mountain Trees, by Robert Preston, or Trees Native to the Forests of Colorado and Wyoming, a U.S. Forest Service information pamphlet.

Leaves occurring singly.
  Leaves flattened, not sharp-pointed.
    Cones numerous, pendent; three-parted bracts
      conspicuous between the cone scales; leaves narrowed
      to a tiny stem . . . . **Douglas-fir** *Pseudotsuga menziesii*
    Cones few, erect, in the top of the tree; no conspicuous
      bracts present; leaves sessile . . . . **Subalpine fir** (fig. 20)
                    Abies lasiocarpa
  Leaves four-angled, sharp-pointed; cones pendent.
    Cones about 2 inches long; leaves acute . . . . **Engelmann spruce**
                  (figs. 9 and 14) *Picea engelmannii*
    Cones 3 to 5 inches long, leaves spine-tipped . . . .
       Colorado blue spruce (figs. 4 and 21) *Picea pungens*
Leaves scalelike or awl-shaped, less than 1 inch long, seeds in
  berrylike cones.
  Leaves scalelike; an erect shrub or small,
    much-branched tree . . . . **Rocky Mountain juniper** (fig. 3)
                   Juniperus scopulorum
  Leaves awl-shaped, spine-tipped; low-spreading shrub . . **Dwarf juniper**
                 Juniperus communis ssp. nana

CATTAIL FAMILY *(TYPHACEAE)*

Everyone is familiar with the tall cattail, *Typha latifolia,* of marshes and pond borders. This is found around a few ponds below 8,000 feet. *Typha angustifolia* is reported to grow at Shadow Mountain Lake.

BUR-REED FAMILY *(SPARGANIACEAE)*

Narrowleaf bur-reed, *Sparganium angustifolium,* is found in Bear Lake and other lakes. It has small white flowers which develop into bur-like clusters of achenes. *Sparganium minimum,* a much smaller plant of similar habit, occurs in some of the ponds.

PONDWEED FAMILY *(NAIADACEAE)*

The **pondweeds** are aquatic plants growing in ponds and slow-moving streams, with two-ranked leaves, the upper firm and floating, the lower submersed and very fragile. *Potamogeton* is the commonest genus. The following species have been identified: *Potamogeton natans, Potamogeton alpinus, Potamageton pusillus,* and *Potamogeton richardsonii.*

WATERPLANTAIN FAMILY *(ALISMATACEAE)*

Plants growing in shallow water or marshy ground with basal, sheathing leaves, and small three-petaled flowers. **American waterplantain,** *Alisma plantago-aquatica,* occurs in marshes and ponds of the park, and **arrowhead,** *Sagittaria cuneata,* a water plant with small white flowers and arrowhead-shaped leaves, is found in Bear, Bierstadt, Sheep, and other lakes.

ARROWGRASS FAMILY *(JUNCAGINACEAE)*

Rushlike plants of marshy ground. **Swamp arrowgrass,** *Triglochin palustre,* and *Triglochin maritimum,* a much larger plant, have been found in swamps of the montane zone.

WATERWEED FAMILY *(HYDROCHARITACEAE)*

A group of water plants, which grow submerged in ponds or lakes, is repre-sented in the park by *Elodea canadensis (Anacharis canadensis),* a plant with oblong or linear, transparent, one-nerved leaves in whorls of three or, on the lower part of the stems, opposite.

GRASS FAMILY *(GRAMINEAE)*

This is one of the largest, most important plant families. Primarily, it fur-nishes all of the bread and cereal foods. Without it, we would not have any meats and dairy products as livestock depend on it. It is important in clothing and buildings. The leaves of grasses form, together with sedges and rushes, the "back-drop" in mountain meadows for plants with conspicuous flowers; however, grasses do not have showy flowers. They are not needed because grasses have developed long filaments on which their anthers are hung so that pollination is accom-plished by the wind.

Grama grass, *Bouteloua gracilis,* erroneously called buffalograss (fig. 22). A small grass recognized by its purplish flaglike inflorescence and curling leaves. It is one of the commonest grasses of the montane region where it forms large mats on the open fields and hillsides and is a valuable pasture grass.

Alpine timothy, *Phleum alpinum.*—A plant with shorter, broader, and more purplish heads than the common timothy is frequent on the mountain meadows.

Many grasses common in the arctic regions, especially species of **bluegrass,** *Poa,* and **fescue,** *Festuca,* are found in the alpine tundra.

Since the grass family is the third largest flowering plant family in the world, it is helpful to group the related genera into tribes. Each tribe has characters that can be generally distinguished in the field. Species of grasses that have been collected in the park are arranged according to tribe in the following list prepared by Dr. Bettie E. Willard:

I. **Fescue Tribe,** *Festuceae:* Inflorescence a panicle, branched several times; more than one floret per spikelet; glumes shorter than the lowest floret of the spikelet (se fig. 3 and definitions in the Glossary).

Bromus carinatus var. *polyanthus*	**Many-flowered brome**
Bromus ciliatus	**Fringed brome**
Bromus inermis	**Smooth brome**
Bromus inermis var. *pumpellianus*	**Pumpelly brome**
Bromus lanatipes	**Woolly nodding brome**
Bromus porteri	**Nodding brome**
Bromus richardsonii	**Richardson brome**
Bromus tectorum	**Cheatgrass**
Festuca baffinensis	**Baffin fescue** (not yet collected in the park, but to be expected)
Festuca brachyphylla	**Alpine fescue**
Festuca elatior	**Meadow fescue**
Festuca idahoensis	**Idaho fescue**
Festuca hallii	**Halls fescue** (rare, but collected just north of the park)
Festuca rubra	**Red fescue**
Festuca saximontana (Festuca ovina)	**Sheep fescue**

Festuca thurberi	**Thurber fescue**
Glyceria borealis	**Northern manna-grass**
Glyceria elata	**Tall manna-grass**
Glyceria maxima ssp. *grandis*	**American manna-grass**
Glyceria striata	**Fowl manna-grass**
Leucopoa kingii (Festuca kingii)	**Spike fescue**
Melica spectabilis	**Purple oniongrass**
Poa agassizensis	**Agassiz bluegrass** (the mountain form of *Poa pratensis*)
Poa alpina	**Alpine bluegrass**
Poa annua	**Annual bluegrass**
Poa arctica	**Arctic bluegrass**
Poa canbyi	**Canby bluegrass**
Poa compressa	**Canada bluegrass**
Poa epilis	**Skyline bluegrass**
Poa fendleriana	**Muttongrass**
Poa glauca	**Timberline bluegrass**
Poa leptocoma	**Bog bluegrass**
Poa lettermanii	**Letterman bluegrass**
Poa nemoralis ssp. *interior*	**Inland bluegrass**
Poa nervosa	**Wheeler bluegrass**
Poa palustris	**Fowl bluegrass**
Poa pattersonii	**Patterson bluegrass**
Poa pratensis	**Kentucky bluegrass**
Poa reflexa	**Nodding bluegrass**
Poa sandbergii	**Sandberg bluegrass**
Torreyochloa pauciflora	**Weak manna-grass** (the type specimen of this grass was collected by Holm on Longs Peak)

II. **Oat Tribe,** *Aveneae:* Inflorescence a panicle; more than one floret to a spikelet; glumes longer than the lowest floret (see fig. 3 of the Glossary).

Avenochloa hookeri	**Spike oat**
Danthonia intermedia	**Timber oatgrass**
Danthonia parryi	**Parry oatgrass**
Deschampsia alpicola	**Alpine hairgrass**
Deschampsia caespitosa	**Tufted hairgrass**
Helictotrichon mortonianum	**Alpine oat**
Koeleria gracilis (Koeleria cristata)	**Junegrass**
Trisetum montanum	**Rocky Mountain trisetum**
Trisetum spicatum	**Spike trisetum**
Trisetum wolfii	**Wolfs trisetum**
Vahlodea atropurpurea	**Mountain hairgrass**

III. **Bentgrass Tribe,** *Agrostideae:* Inflorescence a panicle in most species, but a spike in some; one floret to each spikelet; glumes shorter than the floret (see fig. 3 of the Glossary).

Agrostis bakeri	**Idaho redtop**
Agrostis borealis	**Northern winter bentgrass**
Agrostis exarata	**Spike bentgrass**
Agrostis gigantea	**Redtop**
Agrostis scabra	**Winter redtop, ticklegrass**

Agrostis variabilis	**Ross redtop**
Alopecurus aequalis	**Short-awned foxtail**
Alopecurus alpinus	**Alpine foxtail**
Blepharoneuron tricholepis	**Pine dropseed**
Calamagrostis canadensis	**Canadian reedgrass**
Calamagrostis montanensis	**Plains reedgrass**
Calamagrostis purpurascens	**Purple reedgrass**
Calamagrostis scribneri	**Scribner reedgrass**
Cinna latifolia	**Drooping woodreed**
Muhlenbergia filiformis	**Slender muhly**
Muhlenbergia montana	
Muhlenbergia richardsonis	
Oryzopsis asperifolia	**Roughleaf ricegrass**
Oryzopsis exigua	**Little ricegrass** (collected just north of park)
Oryzopsis micrantha	**Littleseed ricegrass**
Phleum alpinum	**Alpine timothy**
Phleum pratense	**Timothy**
Podagrostis humilis	**Alpine bentgrass**
Podagrostis thurberiana	**Meadow bentgrass**
Stipa columbiana	**Columbia needlegrass**
Stipa comata	**Needle-and-thread**
Stipa lettermanii	**Letterman needlegrass**
Stipa viridula	**Green needlegrass**

IV. **Barley Tribe,** *Hordeae:* Inflorescence a spike, appearing to be unbranched; spikelets sessile on opposite sides of the culm; more than one floret to a spikelet; glumes shorter than the lowest floret (see fig. 3 of the Glossary).

Agropyron albicans var. *griffithsii*	**Griffith wheatgrass**
Agropyron bakeri	**Baker wheatgrass**
Agropyron pauciflorum	**Few-flowered wheatgrass**
Agropyron pseudorepens	**False quackgrass**
Agropyron riparium	**Streambank wheatgrass**
Agropyron scribneri	**Scribner wheatgrass**
Agropyron smithii	**Western wheatgrass**
Agropyron spicatum	**Bluebunch wheatgrass**
Agropyron trachycaulum	**Slender wheatgrass**
Elymus ambiguus	**Colorado wild-rye**
Elymus glaucus	**Blue wild-rye**
Hordeum brachyantherum	**Meadow barley**
Hordeum jubatum	**Foxtail barley**
Sitanion longifolium (Sitanion hystrix)	**Squirreltail**

V. **Windmill Grass Tribe,** *Chlorideae:* Inflorescence unbranched with spikelets all attached on one side of the rachis (see fig. 3 of the Glossary).

Bouteloua gracilis	**Grama grass**
Beckmannia syzigachne	**Sloughgrass**

VI. **Canary Grass Tribe,** *Phalarideae:* Inflorescence a panicle; spikelet with one perfect floret above two staminate florets (see fig. 3 of the Glossary).

Hierochloe odorata	**Sweetgrass**

SEDGE FAMILY *(CYPERACEAE)*

Many members of the sedge family in the genus *Carex* are found in the park. The casual observer often includes them with the grasses, but most sedges may be distinguished from grasses by the shape of their stems, which are usually triangular, and by the absence of nodes or joints in the stems. Sedges are especially abundant in the subalpine meadows and the alpine tundra.

Several sedges are conspicuous for their brown or black, spikelike heads (see fig. 3 of the Glossary). Among these are *Carex aquatilis,* which is a tall plant, 1 to 2 feet high with two to four slender black heads 2 to 3 inches long. *Carex utriculata* is a tall, coarse plant, 1 to 3 feet high, growing in very wet places, such as beaver ponds, in the montane region. This sedge has long, brownish heads up to 3 inches. In the tundra, *Carex scopulorum* dominates wet, snow-free areas. It has jet-black heads that are shorter than those of the plants mentioned above. The following list, prepared by Dr. Bettie E. Willard, shows the species of sedge that have been collected in or near the park:

Carex albonigra
Carex angustior
Carex aquatilis
Carex aquatilis ssp. *stans*
Carex arapahoensis
Carex athrostachya
Carex aurea
Carex bella
Carex brevipes
Carex brunnescens
Carex canescens
Carex capillaris
Carex chalciolepis
Carex disperma
Carex douglasii
Carex ebenea (see fig. 23)
Carex egglestonii
Carex elynoides
Carex festivella
Carex foenea
Carex geyeri
Carex hallii
Carex hassei
Carex haydeniana
Carex heliophila
Carex hoodii
Carex illota
Carex incurviformis
Carex interior
Carex lachenalii

Carex lanuginosa
Carex magellanica ssp. *irrigua*
Carex macloviana
Carex microglochin
Carex microptera
Carex misandra
Carex nebraskensis
Carex nelsonii
Carex nigricans
Carex norvegica
Carex nova
Carex obtusata
Carex occidentalis
Carex oreocharis
Carex perglobosa
Carex petasata
Carex phaeocephala
Carex praeceptorum
Carex praegracilis
Carex praticola
Carex pyrenaica
Carex raynoldsii
Carex rhynchophysa
Carex rossii
Carex rupestris
Carex scopulorum
Carex stenophylla ssp. *eleocharis*
Carex utriculata (Carex rostrata)
Carex vernacula
Carex vesicaria

In the tundra, plants that have the same appearance as *Carex,* but belong to another genus, grow together with alpine sedges. This genus is *Kobresia.* The common species, *Kobresia myosuroides,* is the dominant plant of climax tundra. In autumn, the dense turfs formed by *Kobresia* add a tawny orange color note to the alpine landscape. A rare species, *Kobresia macrocarpa,* has been found on Trail Ridge.

Cottongrass, *Eriophorum angustifolium,* grows in wet meadows and cold bogs of the park where it is quickly seen when in bloom because of its white cottony heads.

Alkali bulrush, *Scirpus paludosus,* grows around some of the ponds. The **few-flowered spikerush,** *Eleocharis pauciflora,* is a common small plant of wet ground. A larger species, *Eleocharis macrostachya,* has been collected near Grand Lake. *Eleocharis acicularis* is found just east of the park.

DUCKWEED FAMILY *(LEMNACEAE)*

Tiny, floating plants, each consisting of a flat, oval, or roundish plant body about ⅛-inch long or less, from one edge of which a slender threadlike root extends into the water. These plants multiply vegetatively, sometimes forming large floating mats. Rarely they produce very simple flowers. **Star duckweed,** *Lemna trisulca* and *Lemna minor,* have been found in the park.

RUSH FAMILY *(JUNCACEAE)*

The rushes have a six-parted perianth, and their flowers are similar in structure to the lilies to which they are related, but their perianths are always small and inconspicuous, usually made up of brownish scales. These plants are grasslike in appearance. The species of the genus *Juncus* have dark green, wiry, tufted, round leaves and stems; they usually grow in wet places. The following species are found in the park:

Juncus arcticus ssp. *ater (Juncus balticus)*	**Arctic rush**
Juncus biglumis	
Juncus castaneus	
Juncus drummondii	
Juncus filiformis	**Drummond rush**
Juncus longistylis	**Short-stemmed rush**
Juncus mertensianus	**Short-styled rush**
Juncus parryi	**Subalpine rush**
Juncus saximontanus	**Parry rush**
Juncus tracyi	**Rocky Mountain rush**
Juncus triglumis	

The woodrushes, species of *Luzula,* have leafy stems and flat grasslike leaves.

Luzula spicata	**Arctic woodrush or spike woodrush**
Luzula parviflora	**Small-flowered woodrush or millet woodrush**
Luzula subcapitata	**Spherical spikerush**

Figure 23. **Ebony sedge.**

Figure 22. **Grama grass.**

Figure 26. **Mariposa-lily.**

Figure 25. **Geyer onion.**

Figure 27. **Snowlily.**

Figure 24. **Nodding onion.**

LILY FAMILY *(LILIACEAE)*

This family is characterized by undivided, parallel-veined leaves and flower parts in three's or sixes. The perianth is made up of segments. These may be all alike or of two kinds corresponding to sepals and petals.

Inflorescence a slender, erect, spikelike raceme, flowers cream. .**Wandlily** (p. 47)
Inflorescence not as above.
    Inflorescence umbellate; flowers pink or whitish. . . . . . .**Wild onion** (p. 46)
    Inflorescence not umbellate.
        Flowers solitary or few, erect, or if bright yellow, nodding; stems
           not branched.
           Flowers white or lavender-tinged.
               Plant stemless; flower pure white; growing on open fields at low
                   altitudes; blooming in early spring. . . . .**Sandlily** (p. 47)
               Plant with slender stem.
                   Flower 1 inch long or less; alpine zone; petals
                      purple-veined. . . . .**Alplily** (p. 47)
                   Flower usually 2 inches long or more; petals with dark
                      splotches at base. . . . .**Mariposa-lily** (p. 46)
            Flowers red or yellow.
               Flowers bright yellow, nodding. . . . .**Snowlily** (p. 47)
               Flowers red or orange, erect. . . . .**Mountain woodlily** (p. 47)
        Flowers few or many; plant leafy-stemmed.
            Stem branched.
               Flowers few, terminal, ripening into
                   red berries. . . . .**Fairybells** (p. 47)
               Flowers axillary, pendent, ripening into
                   red berries. . . . .**Twisted-stalk** (p. 47)
            Stem unbranched; flowers in a
               terminal raceme. . . . .**Star solomonplume** (p. 47)

Wild onion, *Allium.*—Plants from bulbs with slender basal leaves and leafless stems bearing terminal umbels of white or rose-colored flowers. Perianth segments all alike. Foliage with a distinct onion smell when bruised. The different species may be distinguished by the following key:

Umbels nodding, flowers pink or whitish, bulb coat not netted. .**Nodding onion**
Umbels not nodding, bulb coat netted or fibrous.
    Flowers rose-purple; plants of montane and subalpine meadows.
        Perianth segments acute. . . . .**Geyer onion**
        Perianth segments long acuminate. . . . .**Short-styled onion**

Nodding onion, *Allium cernuum* (fig. 24), with pale pink or purplish flowers, is common on fields and hillsides of the montane and subalpine regions. **Geyer onion,** *Allium geyeri* (fig. 25), and the **short-styled onion,** *Allium brevistylum,* both with purple blossoms, occur in meadows of the same regions.

Allium textile has been reported.

Mariposa-lily, *Calochortus gunnisonii* (fig. 26).—One of the most beautiful plants of the park, blooming in early summer. The large tuliplike white or lavender flowers are borne on a slender stem. Perianth segments are of two kinds—three broad petals with dark splotches at their bases and three narrow sepals. The leaves are narrow and tapering. These plants are most commonly found near the edges of moist aspen thickets and in meadows.

Snowlily, *Erythronium grandflorum* ssp. *chrysandrum* (fig. 27).—A striking plant with bright yellow flowers, blooming as the snow melts in the subalpine zone. The six-pointed petals are recurved. Leaves, only two and basal. This plant is frequent in Wild Basin, on Specimen Mountain, and on the western slope. It follows the snow up the slopes, and all stages, from ripened seed to pointed shoots just breaking the ground, may be found in a climb of from 9,000 to 11,000 feet.

Sandlily, *Leucocrinum montanum.*—A snow-white lily blooming close to the ground in early spring. The leaves are long and narrow and the flowers without stems. This plant is abundant on the plains and eastern foothills where it blooms in April. It is found in May around Estes Park, but it is seldom found at a higher altitude.

Mountain woodlily, *Lilium philadelphicum (Lilium montanum)* (fig. 28).— A rare, beautiful plant of the montane meadows and moist thickets with erect goblet-shaped orange-red blossoms 3 or 4 inches deep. The upper leaves are in whorls.

Alplily, *Lloydia serotina* (fig. 29).—A slender plant of the alpine zone, usually blooming rather early in the season. The petals and sepals are creamy-white, veined with purple, sometimes tinged with pink on the outside. Stem 2 to 8 inches high. It is most abundant on exposed rocky slopes.

Wandlily or **mountain deathcamas,** *Zygadenus elegans* (fig. 30).—Flowers several in a spikelike raceme, cream-colored; petals and sepals alike, each with a greenish or yellowish spot. Plants growing in meadows at all altitudes. In the alpine zone, a dwarf form is common. This plant is somewhat poisonous but less so than are the other species of the genus, which are found at lower altitudes and sometimes cause the death of sheep and cattle.

Fairybells, *Disporum trachycarpum.*—Flowers greenish or yellowish, inconspicuous; fruit a bright red, three-lobed berry, at the tips of the branches. This has been found in Wild Basin and along the Cub Lake Trail.

Star solomonplume, *Smilacina stellata* (fig. 31).—A frequent plant of the montane and subalpine zones with a terminal raceme of small, star-shaped white flowers ripening into mottled berries. The leaves are alternate and sessile. Two forms of this plant occur—a slender dark green type with flat leaves in shady moist situations and a stouter, dwarf form, yellowish-green and with leaves more or less folded, in dry and sunny situations. *Smilacina racemosa,* another kind of solomonplume with smaller but more numerous flowers in a panicle, occurs in moist, shaded areas. These plants are related to the eastern solomonseal but differ from it in having their flowers terminal and stems never branched. They have been called false solomonseal.

Twisted-stalk, *Streptopus amplexifolius.*—A plant 2 to 4 feet high, frequent in moist areas of the upper montane and subalpine forests. It may be distinguished from the solomonplume by the branching stem and axillary, pendent blossoms which ripen into red berries.

Figure 29. **Alplily.**

Figure 28. **Mountain woodlily.**

Figure 30. **Wandlily.**

Figure 31. **Solomonplume.**

Figure 32. **Rocky Mountain iris.**

Figure 33. **Blue-eyed-grass.**

IRIS FAMILY *(IRIDACEAE)*

This family is related to the lily family and has parallel-veined leaves; sepals, petals, stamens, and divisions of the seedpod—three each. The seedpod is inferior, that is, the corolla and other flower parts are on top of it.

Rocky Mountain iris, *Iris missouriensis* (fig. 32).—Common in meadows and moist situations of the montane zone. The flower may be easily recognized by its similarity to the garden irises. The meadows in Moraine Park, Horseshoe Park, and along the Devils Gulch and Longs Peak roads are often blue with these charming flowers in June.

Blue-eyed grass, *Sisyrinchium occidentale* (fig. 33).—A plant with grasslike leaves and small, bright blue flowers found in wet meadows. The flowers open only when the sun is shining.

ORCHID FAMILY *(ORCHIDACEAE)*

This is one of the most highly specialized families of plants. The stamens and pistil are grown together and the flower is irregular. The lower petal is usually developed into a sac or spur and is called the *lip.* All flowers in the orchid family are so constructed that in order to produce seed they must be pollinated by insects.

AA. Flowers conspicuous; lip inflated.
    B. Flowers yellow; plant 8 inches high or over . . **Yellow ladyslipper** (p. 49)
    BB. Flowers not yellow.
        a. Flowers rose-purple, solitary . . . . **Fairy slipper** (p. 49)
        aa. Flowers dull purplish or brownish,
            usually two or more on each stem . . . **Brownie ladyslipper** (p. 51)
AA. Flowers usually inconspicuous, white or greenish.
    B. Plant reddish-brown or yellow except for the
        flowers, no green leaves present . . . . **Coralroot** (p. 51)
    BB. Plant always with green leaves.
        a. Leaves dark green mottled
            with white . . . . **Western rattlesnake-plantain** (p. 51)
        aa. Leaves bright, even green.
            b. Leaves only one or two.
                c. Leaf one, near base of stem . . . . . . **One-leaved orchid** (p. 51)
                cc. Leaves two, opposite, halfway up stem . . . **Twayblade** (p. 51)
            bb. Leaves several, flowers in spikes.
                c. Spike spirally twisted . . . . **Ladies-tresses** (p. 51)
                cc. Spike not spirally twisted . . . . **Bog orchid** (p. 51)

Fairy slipper or **calypso,** *Calypso bulbosa* (fig. 34).—A dainty little orchid with rose-colored, slipperlike flower found in June in moist pine and spruce woods and along shady streams.

Yellow ladyslipper, *Cypripedium calceolus* (fig. 35).—One of the rarest and most beautiful plants in the Rocky Mountains. *Blossoms of this plant should not be picked as it is in danger of extermination.* This is a leafy-stemmed plant about 1 foot in height. The flower has a large yellow lip, 1 to 2 inches in length, and greenish-yellow, twisted sepals.

Figure 35. **Yellow ladyslipper.**

Figure 34. **Fairy slipper.**

Figure 37. **Spotted coralroot.**

Figure 36. **Brownie ladyslipper.**

Figure 38. **Heart-leaved twayblade.**

Brownie ladyslipper, *Cypripedium fasciculatum* (fig. 36).—A small plant with only two leaves on each stem and several inconspicuous dark-reddish or yellowish flowers, frequently found in the spruce forests of the subalpine region. It grows singly or in clumps.

Spotted coralroot, *Corallorhiza maculata* (fig. 37).—A saprophytic plant without green leaves growing in coniferous forests of the montane and subalpine zones. The brownish stem bears several dainty flowers with purplish-spotted petals. Another species, **little yellow coralroot,** *Corallorhiza trifida,* occurs along wet banks and the rare **spring coralroot,** *Corallorhiza wisteriana,* has been found in Forest Canyon.

Ladies-tresses, *Spiranthes romanzoffiana.*—A small plant rarely over 8 inches high with light green foliage and a twisted, crowded spike of pure white, fragrant blossoms. It is frequent in the subalpine region where it is often found growing in moss, especially around Nymph Lake, in bogs along the Loch Vale Trail, and along the North and East Inlet streams. It blooms in late summer.

Western rattlesnake-plantain, *Goodyera oblongifolia (Goodyera decipiens.)*—A plant of moist, coniferous forests, with mottled leaves, all basal, and a spike of inconspicuous greenish flowers. Flower stem 4 to 8 inches high.

White bog-orchid, *Habenaria dilatata.*—A slender plant 1 to 2 feet high, bearing a spike of white flowers with narrow petals, the lower elongated backward into a slender spur. The **northern green bog-orchid,** *Habenaria hyperborea,* a stouter plant with green blossoms and the **bracted bog-orchid,** *Habenaria viridis* var. *bracteata,* with toothed lip are also found. All three grow in the bogs and meadows of the subalpine region and are especially abundant around Bear Lake. The **one-leaved orchid,** *Habenaria obtusata,* is occasionally found in wet coniferous woods. It may be recognized by its one obtuse leaf.

Heart-leaved twayblade, *Listera cordata* (fig. 38), and **northern twayblade,** *Listera convallarioides,* are inconspicuous plants of mossy or wet shaded banks. They are easily recognized by the two broad, opposite leaves placed about the middle of the stem. The shape of the lip petal distinguishes the two species. In the former, it is divided halfway to the base into two narrow-pointed lobes. In the latter, it is wedgeshaped with two short-rounded lobes.

WILLOW FAMILY *(SALICACEAE)*

Nearly all of the non-evergreen trees and many of the shrubs seen in the park belong to this family. The leaves of these are always alternate and simple, never compound, lobed, or cut. They grow on moist ground, often along watercourses.

Poplars or **cottonwoods,** *Populus.*—The buds on trees of this genus are always covered by several overlapping scales.

Narrowleaf cottonwood, *Populus angustifolia.*—Very abundant along the streams in the montane region and below. This tree is striking in the autumn, when the leaves turn a brilliant orange-yellow.

Balsam poplar, *Populus balsamifera.*—A rare tree in the park. A few are found along the lower part of Fern Lake Trail, in Horseshoe Park, and in Wild Basin. It may be distinguished from the narrowleaf cottonwood by its larger and more fragrant sticky buds and broader, ovate leaf.

Quaking aspen, *Populus tremuloides* (fig. 39).—The commonest broadleaved tree in the park. It is found throughout the upper montane and subalpine zones. In moist, sheltered situations and on good soil, it develops beautiful groves of tall, straight white-barked trees. On rocky slopes or on poor soil, it forms scrubby thickets. The petiole is flattened at right angles to the blade of the leaf, which enables the leaves to move with the slightest breeze, and this habit gives the trees their name of **quaking aspen.** Some of these trees will be found along nearly all watercourses and ravines in the park. When they put on their autumn coloring, every big and little ravine stands out, a stream of flame or gold color, in vivid contrast to the dark green of the surrounding coniferous forest.

Willow, *Salix.*—The willows of the park are numerous in species and abundant as individuals. They border the streams in all the lower valleys, form dense thickets in the subalpine zone, spread over the moist swales at timberline as knee-deep carpets, and creep as tiny dwarfs among the stones of the alpine regions. They are subject to diseases which cause them to die back periodically, but when in good condition, they contribute in all seasons to the beauty of the region. The gray tones of their leafless twigs merging into yellow, reds, and bronzes, which become intensified with the approach of the growing season, give life to the winter picture; in spring, several species display typical "pussy willow" catkins, their flower buds. As the flowers develop and these silvery "kittens" extend into catkins with yellow-anthered stamens increasing their size and conspicuousness, some of these shrubs are really handsome. Then comes the early green of their leaves while other shrubs and trees are still dormant. During the summer, different species show subtle differences in color, bright greens, and silvery effects. As autumn approaches, their foliage becomes a mantle of gold and russet, ripening and falling to merge with the accumulation of vegetation, which helps build up the bogs into meadows, forming spongy humus-filled soil.

In addition to their contribution to the beauty of the landscape, they serve wildlife in many ways. Beaver almost entirely depend on them for food in areas where aspen are not available, and they are used extensively in the dams. Elk and deer browse their bud-laden twigs and rest in the protection of their dense thickets. Many smaller mammals and birds, notably the ptarmigan, find both food and shelter in all types of willow growth.

Members of this genus may always be easily identified by the single bud-scale which covers each bud like a little hood. In some species, when the bud begins to expand this scale is simply pushed up where it perches temporarily as a small cap. The differentiation of individual species of *Salix* is much more difficult.

The commonest tall willow is the **mountain willow,** *Salix monticola* (9 to 18 feet), found along the streams about Estes Park and sometimes up to 9,000 feet. **Scouler willow,** *Salix scouleriana,* is a shrub or small tree, found along streams, with exceptionally large, oval or roundish, staminate catkins, from ¾ to 1-¾ inches long and ¾-inch wide, blooming before the leaves appear. The staminate bushes are conspicuous in May or early June, depending on altitude and season, when each shrub becomes a mass of pale yellow from the pollen-laden anthers of the catkins. This one may be distinguished by the appressed, reddish hairs on the undersides of the leaves. This species is seen at Bear Lake, Dream Lake, and along Trail Ridge Road. While it is common in moist locations, it is the one species most likely to be found in drier situations, such as the drier meadows and occasionally up on hillsides. **Bebb willow,** *Salix bebbiana,* is naturally a tall shrub (on the Wild Basin Trail it reaches 25 feet) with very small leaves, distinctly netted on the under side. However, in the open parks, such as Horseshoe Park, it is often browsed down to only 2 or 3 feet. The commonest species found below 8,000 feet about Estes Park village, Beaver Point, and Grand Lake, is the **caudate-leaved willow,** *Salix caudata.* This grows 6 to 12 feet tall and has shining reddish or reddish-yellow twigs.

The **silver pussy willow** of the park is *Salix subcoerulea (Salix drummondiana).* This shrub grows 3 to 12 feet tall; its smooth purplish-brown branches are often frosted with a silvery bloom; its leaves are silvery-silky; and its large silvery catkins appear before the leaves unfold. The anthers are red before shedding the pollen. *Salix irrorata,* another handsome pussy willow, is found in canyons below 6,000 feet.

The **planeleaf willow,** *Salix planifolia,* is very abundant and represented by two varieties, the **subalpine willow,** *Salix planifolia* var. *monica* (figs. 40 and 41) and **Nelson willow,** *Salix planifolia* var. *nelsonii.* Both forms extend over a wide range in altitude. They are bushy, much-branched shrubs with dark shining twigs and dark green leaves shining above but glaucous beneath. Many of the dwarf willow thickets at higher altitudes are made up mainly of these two, although the Nelson willow is also found growing 8 to 10 feet tall at lower stations, such as Beaver Point.

One of the most interesting groups of plants in the whole park is that comprising the alpine creeping willows. These are woody plants with "trunks" sometimes an inch or more in diameter and often buried in the ground, and prostrate branches. Only short branchlets, from less than 1 to sometimes 3 inches high, stand erect. The **creeping willow,** *Salix arctica* (fig. 42), may be recognized by its dark green shiny leaves, pale beneath, which have distinctly yellow petioles.

The **cascade willow,** *Salix cascadensis,* is rare in this area, commoner in the northern Rockies, but may be found on Trail Ridge. It has slenderer stems than the creeping willow, and its leaves are light green on both surfaces. **Snow willow,** *Salix nivalis,* is one of the tiniest. Its leaves are shining and strongly netted-veined above, glaucous beneath, with in-rolled margins and yellowish petioles. The **Rocky Mountain snow willow,** *Salix reticulata var. nivalis,* is much commoner and larger, its branches may be up to 4 inches high with leaves paler and less shining but otherwise similar.

The alpine slopes between Fall River Pass and Poudre Lakes are excellent places to see these miniature willows. Many of the larger forms may be found here as well.

In addition, the following species have been identified in this area: *Salix barclayi, Salix brachycarpa, Salix geyeriana, Salix petiolaris, Salix pseudocordata, Salix padophylla, Salix pseudolapponum, Salix serissima, Salix wolfii, Salix glauca,* and *Salix exigua.*

BIRCH FAMILY *(BETULACEAE)*

Shrubs or small trees found along streams or on wet ground. Their flowers are in catkins, and their leaves have toothed margins.

Water birch, *Betula occidentalis (Betula fontinalis).*—A large, graceful shrub with smooth reddish-brown bark and drooping branches, frequent along streams in the montane region. The leaves are thin, ovate, and serrate. In some seasons, these birches turn a beautiful clear yellow in the autumn.

Bog birch, *Betula glandulosa.*—Abundant in the lower alpine and the subalpine regions and occasionally found lower. A dwarf, much-branched shrub with small, roundish toothed leaves; very common in meadows and along streams in the timberline region.

Thinleaf alder, *Alnus tenuifolia.*—A small tree of shrublike growth with gray bark and rather large distinctly veined and double-toothed leaves. Abundant along streams. The trunks are often 4 to 8 inches in diameter.

NETTLE FAMILY *(URTICACEAE)*

The common **tall nettle,** *Urtica dioica* ssp. *gracilis,* has been found on waste ground and along roadsides.

MISTLETOE FAMILY *(LORANTHACEAE)*

The members of this family are all parasites. Those growing in the park are inconspicuous and belong to the group called the **lesser mistletoe.**

Pine mistletoe. — Yellowish-brown or greenish woody plants with scalelike leaves, inconspicuous flowers, and sticky berries, growing as parasites on members of the pine family. *Arceuthobium vaginatum* is the most frequently seen. It has orange-brown stems and occurs commonly on ponderosa pine; *Arceuthobium americanum* has whorled branching and occurs mainly on lodgepole but sometimes on limber pine. On lodgepole pine also is *Arceuthobium campylopodum,* which has a fanlike branching. It also sometimes occurs on ponderosa pine. *Arceuthobium douglasii* occurs on Douglas-fir.

The mistletoe results in the development of "witches brooms" on the trees, which it attacks and finally may cause the death of the tree. The sticky seeds are carried by birds to other trees, where they germinate and produce new plants.

BUCKWHEAT FAMILY *(POLYGONACEAE)*

This family is characterized either by having the flowers in umbels subtended by involucres (as in the sulphur flowers), or by having the stipules membranous and sheathing the stem (as in the docks and knotweeds). Most plants of this family have triangular achenes.

Figure 39. **Quaking aspen, leaves.**

Figure 40. **Subalpine willow, about 1 foot tall, beginning to bloom in June near small tundra pond.**

Figure 41. **Subalpine willow, detail of catkins.**

Figure 42. **Creeping willow, erect stems not over an inch tall, catkins.**

Figure 43. **Sulphur flower.**

Figure 44. **Water buckwheat.**

A. Plant 1 to 2 feet tall; inflorescence much branched; leaves all basal, seeds triangular winged......................**Winged buckwheat** (p. 56)
AA. Plant usually less than 1 foot tall.
  B. Flowers in umbels with subtending involucres.
    a. Plants dwarf and matted; leaves white, woolly; alpine zone.......
      Alpine golden buckwheat (p. 56)
    aa. Plants erect, flower stems over 3 inches high.
      b. Flowers deep yellow, turning reddish in drying.
        c. Perianth smooth, plant very abundant on montane fields...
          Sulphur flower (p. 56)
        cc. Perianth hairy, plant rare.......**Golden buckwheat** (p. 56)
      bb. Flowers cream-colored, sometimes with reddish tinge; subalpine and alpine zones.............**Subalpine buckwheat** (p. 56)
  BB. Flowers not in umbels.
    a. Flowers in the axils; leaves with papery, sheathing bases.
      b. Plant climbing by means of a twining stem; leaves heart-shaped
        Black bindweed (p. 57)
      bb. Plants not climbing.
        c. Plant flat and matlike; leaves oblong; dooryards and roadsides ....**Dooryard knotweed** (p. 57)
        cc. Plant with erect or ascending stems; leaves long and narrow
          Knotweed (p. 57)
    aa. Flowers in dense panicles, spikes, or heads.
      b. Flowers never white nor brilliant rose color.
        c. Plants less than 1 foot high; leaves acid flavored.
          d. Leaves roundish or heart-shaped; subalpine or alpine among rocks.................**Alpine sorrel** (p. 57)
          dd. Leaves halberd-shaped; plants of roadsides and waste ground......................**Sheep sorrel** (p. 57)
        cc. Plants 1 to 3 feet high with stout stems and large leaves...
          Dock (p. 57)
      bb. Flowers white, pinkish, or rose.
        c. Plant aquatic; flowers brilliant rose......................
          Water buckwheat (p. 57)
        cc. Plants not aquatic; flowers white or tinged pinkish........
          Bistort (p. 57)

Winged buckwheat, *Eriogonum alatum.*—A silky hairy plant 1 to 3 feet high, branched above, with long, narrow, mostly basal leaves, rounded at the tips; frequently found on the montane fields. The triangular seeds are winged.

Sulphur flower, *Eriogonum umbellatum* (fig. 43).—Very abundant on montane fields and hillsides, easily recognized by its umbrella-like clusters of small smooth yellow flowers and its woolly, entire leaves. These flowers often turn reddish late in the season.

Alpine golden buckwheat, *Eriogonum flavum.*—This resembles the sulphur flower in appearance but is much less frequent. It may be distinguished by the hairy perianth. It is a matted, dwarf plant, with small flower-heads, found in dry places above timberline.

Subalpine buckwheat, *Eriogonum subalpinum.*—A flower very similar to the sulphur flower but cream-colored instead of yellow; in maturity, it has a reddish tinge. Found abundantly in the subalpine zone.

Black bindweed, *Polygonum convolvulus.*—A climbing plant with heart-shaped leaves and inconspicuous flowers occasionally found on waste ground.

Dooryard knotweed, *Polygonum aviculare.*—A common weed introduced from Europe; found around dwellings. It is a low, spreading plant with pinkish green blossoms and black, shiny three-angled seeds.

The following species of knotweed, with blossoms and seeds similar to the dooryard knotweed, are found in the park: *Polygonum douglasii, Polygonum engelmannii, Polygonum kelloggii, Polygonum montanum,* and *Polygonum minimum.* The latter is a small plant with crowded leaves and is apparently quite rare. Seed-eating birds are seen in late summer, autumn, and winter busily feeding on knotweed seeds.

Alpine sorrel, *Oxyria digyna.*—A smooth, rather fleshy plant with roundish leaves, found in the wet places among rocks of the alpine and subalpine regions in the park and around the Northern Hemisphere. Many greenish flowers, the sepals tinged with red. The leaves of this plant are pleasantly acid and may be used to flavor the hiker's lunch.

Sheep sorrel, *Rumex acetosella.*—A weed introduced from Europe, having leaves with two sharp lobes at the base, like a spearhead, and dense panicles of small reddish flowers; grows around dwellings and along roadsides. It is the "sour grass" of the East.

Curly dock, *Rumex crispus,* and **Mexican dock,** *Rumex salicifolius* ssp. *triangulivalvis.*—Both stout weeds with dense panicles of greenish blossoms. *Rumex densiflorus,* with valves without callosites and large leaves, often a foot or more in length, is found along streams or on wet ground.

Water buckwheat or **water ladysthumb,** *Polygonum amphibium* (fig. 44).—Growing in water, sometimes in mud, with bright rose-colored blossom spikes. This has been found in some of the montane lakes.

American bistort, *Polygonum bistortoides (Bistorta bistortoides)* (fig. 45).—A plant of wet ground, 8 inches to 2 feet high, with a short, oblong, dense spike of white flowers sometimes tinged pinkish. Leaves narrow, entire, and mostly basal. **Alpine bistort,** *Polygonum viviparum (Bistorta vivipara),* a much smaller plant with elongated, slender spike, in which some of the blossoms are replaced by bulblets that are its only means of reproduction, is frequent in moist places of the subalpine and alpine regions. This plant also occurs in arctic America, Europe, and Asia.

Koenigia, *Koenigia islandica.*—A diminutive arctic-alpine annual with white blossoms has been found at several places in the park. It is less than 1 inch tall when mature. The plants look like tiny seedlings and grow in shallow running water or wet moss on the tundra.

GOOSEFOOT FAMILY *(CHENOPODIACEAE)*

A family of weeds and vegetables. Most of the wild species are considered weeds, but the family includes many garden vegetables, such as spinach, beets, and chard.

Squaw paint or **strawberry blite,** *Chenopodium capitatum* (fig. 46).—A plant with conspicuous deep-red, berrylike clusters of small flowers, and leaves with spear-shaped or heart-shaped bases. It is occasionally seen along roadsides and on rich soil. **Fremont chenopod,** *Chenopodium fremontii,* a branching plant, 1 to 2 feet tall with triangular-shaped leaves and inconspicuous flowers, grows among bushes on open slopes of the montane region and is a very good cattle food.

The other members of this family found in the park are weedy plants growing along roadsides and on waste ground. The following species occur: **lambsquarters,** *Chenopodium album,* and *Chenopodium berlandieri,* **monolepis,** *Monolepis nuttalliana,* and **tumbling Russianthistle,** *Salsola kali.*

AMARANTH FAMILY *(AMARANTHACEAE)*

A family containing many troublesome weeds, most of which are not native in this country.

Redroot amaranth, *Amaranthus retroflexus.*—A stout weed with crowded spikes of small, inconspicuous greenish flowers interspersed with spine-tipped bracts, growing along roadsides and on waste ground.

FOUR-O'CLOCK FAMILY *(NYCTAGINACEAE)*

The plants of this family derive their name from the habit of their flowers of opening late in the afternoon.

Wild four-o'clock, *Oxybaphus hirsutus.*—A purplish hairy plant with clusters of small flowers, surrounded by an involucre. Perianth pink or purplish. Found around Estes Park village and in rocky places of the montane zone.

PURSLANE FAMILY *(PORTULACACEAE)*

This family may be recognized by the very thin and delicate petals, either white, pink, or purple, and the two sepals, together with smooth and entire leaves.

Lanceleaf springbeauty, *Claytonia lanceolata* (fig. 47).—A plant with delicate pale pink blossoms often with darker veins and a pair of smooth, entire leaves on the stems. This usually has no basal leaf. The flowers open only in the sun and last but a day. Frequent on moist ground. It is quite abundant in Wild Basin, blooming around the snowbanks. *Claytonia rosea* is similar but has narrower leaves and usually one or more basal leaves. It is common on the eastern foothills, blooming in early spring.

Big-rooted springbeauty, Claytonia megarhiza (fig. 48).—A high alpine plant growing in rock crevices with a very large purple taproot, which often reaches to a great depth, and many white or pink flowers with pinkish veins.

Pygmy bitterroot, *Lewisia pygmaea* (fig. 49).—A small plant of the alpine and subalpine regions with linear leaves and delicate rose-red to white flowers. The two sepals have gland-tipped teeth, which give them a minutely beaded appearance. **Bitterroot,** *Lewisia rediviva,* the Montana State flower, occurs on gravelly mesas near Granby. The genus to which these plants belong was named in honor of Capt. Meriwether Lewis of the Lewis and Clark Expedition.

Water springbeauty, *Montia chamissoi.*—A weak-stemmed plant with fragile white flowers and opposite leaves, found along streams and in wet places.

Figure 45. **American bistort.**

Figure 48. **Big-rooted springbeauty.**

Figure 46. **Squaw paint.**

Figure 49. **Pygmy bitterroot.**

Figure 50. **Fendler sandwort.**

Figure 47. **Lanceleaf springbeauty.**

PINK FAMILY *(CARYOPHYLLACEAE)*

Opposite leaves and enlarged nodes are characteristics of this family. The petals are usually notched or split part way to the base. Most species are white-flowered; a few are pink or reddish.

A. Sepals united, forming a tubular or ovoid, 10-ribbed calyx.
  B. Styles three.....................................**Silene** (p. 61)
  BB. Styles five....................................**Lychnis** (p. 61)
AA. Sepals distinct or nearly so.
  B. Petals deeply notched or two-cleft.
    a. Styles usually three; plants usually smooth, never sticky.........
    Chickweed (p. 60)
    aa. Styles usually five; plants soft pubescent, often sticky above.....
    Mouse-ear chickweed (p. 60)
  BB. Petals entire or very slightly notched or lacking.
    a. Petals lacking.............................**Nailwort** (p. 61)
    aa. Petals present.
      b. Styles five........................**Arctic pearlwort** (p. 61)
      bb. Styles three.
        c. Leaves narrow, rigid, sharp-pointed.......**Sandwort** (p. 60)
        cc. Leaves oblong, blunt at tip..**Blunt-leaved chickweed** (p. 60)

Fendler sandwort, *Arenaria fendleri* (fig. 50).—A tufted plant with narrow, rigid grasslike leaves and few to many white flowers with red or dark-colored anthers. Abundant in the montane and subalpine zones on hillsides and under pine trees. A dwarf form is sometimes found above timberline. The plant is sticky in the inflorescence.

Equal-stemmed sandwort, *Arenaria rubella.*—A small tufted plant apparently rather rare, with threadlike stems of nearly equal height, bearing small white flowers. The sepals are strongly three-nerved and longer than the petals. The leaves are crowded at the base, narrowly awl-shaped and semicylindric.

Alpine sandwort, *Arenaria obtusiloba* (fig. 51).—A mosslike plant starred with comparatively large white blossoms, found in the alpine region among rocks and on sandy, snow-free ground where it is very abundant.

Snowbed sandwort, *Arenaria sajanensis.*—Found in snow accumulation areas of the tundra. Very much like the alpine sandwort, but with a looser mat and smaller flowers.

Blunt-leaved chickweed, *Arenaria lateriflora.*—Found in similar places, may be distinguished from species of *Stellaria* by its oblong, obtuse leaves and its usually obtuse sepals.

Mouse-ear chickweed or **cerastium,** *Cerastium.*—The scientific name of this genus is a Greek derivative and means "little horn" in reference to the shape of the seedpod which suggests a powderhorn. The small downy leaves give it its name of "mouse ear." This hairiness and the larger blossoms distinguish these plants from the true chickweeds of the genus *Stellaria*. The park's species of *Cerastium* are difficult to distinguish and are found in all zones. The common white flower, ½-inch broad or less, with hairy-sticky stem, cleft petals, and narrow, pointed leaves, found frequently on moist hillsides of the montane zone in May and June, is *Cerastium arvense.* In the alpine region, *Cerastium beeringianum* ssp. *earlei,* is frequent. *Cerastium vulgatum* has been found in the Never Summers.

Mountain pink or **campion,** *Lychnis montana (Melandrium apetalum).*—A dwarf, compact plant of the alpine zone with one-flowered stems 4 inches or less in height; calyx somewhat inflated and petals short, nearly or completely included in the calyx. It is not frequent. A similar but rarer plant of the tundra is *Lychnis kingii (Melandrium furcatum),* having tiny white flowers.

White cockle or **evening campion,** *Lychnis alba.*—A stout hairy weed with conspicuous white flowers, introduced around buildings and ranches. The flowers open at night. These plants are polygamo-dioecious.

Drummond cockle, *Lychnis drummondii.*—A slender plant of moist places, usually in the subalpine zone, with flowers one to five, petals reddish (rarely whitish), and calyx with 10 dark stripes. At least the upper part of the stem is sticky.

Moss campion, *Silene acaulis* (fig. 52).—A mossy, cushion-like plant with conspicuous pink flowers, abundant among rocks in the tundra. It is found in alpine-arctic situations from New Hampshire to New Mexico and to Alaska, also in Greenland and Eurasia.

Halls catchfly, *Silene hallii.*—A sticky, weedy-looking plant with dirty-white or cream-colored blossoms, frequently found in the aspen groves of the montane zone.

The **chickweeds** or **starworts,** slender, smooth little plants with small white starlike blossoms and pointed leaves and sepals, are frequently found in moist situations. The following species occur, especially in the subalpine and alpine region: *Stellaria crassifolia, Stellaria longifolia, Stellaria umbellata, Stellaria longipes,* and *Stellaria laeta.*

Arctic pearlwort, *Sagina saginoides.*—A tiny inconspicuous plant with narrow leaves and small flowers on very slender stems, found above 12,000 feet on Trail Ridge; probably elsewhere.

Rocky Mountain nailwort, *Paronychia sessiliflora* ssp. *pulvinata.*—A tiny cushionlike plant of exposed mountaintops with very inconspicuous flowers, having awn-tipped sepals and no petals, occasionally found in the alpine region. **James nailwort,** *Paronychia jamesii,* has been found near Glen Haven.

WATERLILY FAMILY *(NYMPHACEAE)*

A family of aquatic plants with showy blossoms and large floating leaves. Only one species is found in the park. These plants are not true lilies. They are more nearly related to the buttercups, as their flower arrangement indicates.

Yellow pondlily or **Rocky Mountain cowlily,** *Nuphar luteum* ssp. *polysepalum (Nymphaea polysepala)* (fig. 53).—A plant with yellow flowers 2 to 3 inches across, blooming in July and August. In some lakes between 9,000 and 10,000 feet altitude.

Figure 51. **Alpine sandwort, plant cushionlike.**

Figure 52. **Moss campion.**

Figure 53. **Yellow pondlily, flowers 2 - 3 inches broad.**

Figure 54. **White marsh-marigold.**

Figure 55. **Globeflower, flower 1 - 2 inches broad.**

Figure 56. **American pasqueflower.**

BUTTERCUP FAMILY *(RANUNCULACEAE)*

This family is a very large one and contains many of the park's most beautiful wildflowers. It is characterized by having an indefinite number, usually several, of stamens and pistils, and by having the stamens, sepals, and petals, when present, inserted below the pistils. It includes a great many plants of widely differing appearance. The buttercup order is believed to include the most primitive of seed plants now living and is considered by many botanists to be the trunk of the family tree of the seed plants from which the more highly specialized groups have branched off at different times through the ages. Many of the most showy garden plants belong to this group, including the *Ranunculus, Anemone, Delphinium, Paonia* (peony), and *Aquilegia* (columbine).

Plants climbing or trailing, stems woody...................**Clematis** (p. 67)
Plants erect, never climbing or trailing; stems herbaceous.
    Leaves compound, made up of numerous, roundish,
      usually lobed leaflets.
        Flowers conspicuous, petals spurred..............**Columbine** (p. 68)
        Flowers inconspicuous; stamens numerous, long....**Meadowrue** (p. 67)
    Leaves simple, divided or compound but never composed
      of roundish leaflets.
      Flowers regular.
        Flowers in spikelike racemes, ripening into white
          or red berries.............................**Baneberry** (p. 70)
        Flowers never in spikelike racemes; fruit not berrylike.
          Flowers with only one cycle of perianth segments present,
            these usually petallike.
            Plants with silky or hairy foliage
              and stems........................**Anemone** (p. 67)
            Plants with smooth foliage and stems.
              Leaves entire, all basal.........**Marsh-marigold** (p. 63)
              Leaves much divided; stem leafy....**Globeflower** (p. 63)
          Flowers with two cycles in the perianth,
            both sepals and petals..............**Buttercup** (pp. 64, 66)
      Flowers irregular, mostly dark blue, rarely pale or whitish.
        Upper sepal spurred.........................**Larkspur** (p. 68)
        Upper sepal helmet-shaped..................**Monkshood** (p. 68)

Mousetail, *Myosurus minimus (Myosurus aristatus).*—A diminutive plant growing in mud, with a tuft of narrow leaves and small white blossoms, with numerous pistils which form a cylindric spike of achenes when mature. It has been found on wet ground in the vicinity of Longs Peak.

White marsh-marigold, *Caltha leptosepala* (fig. 54).—Abundant in swampy places of the subalpine and alpine zones. Its oblong and narrowly oval sepals vary from five to 15 in number. They are white inside, sometimes tinged with bluish outside. The anthers of the numerous stamens give the flower a conspicuous yellow center. It has several pistils which develop into a cluster of small green pods. The leaves, all basal, are 1 to 4 inches long, entire and usually oval, with a somewhat heart-shaped base.

Globeflower, *Trollius laxus* var. *albiflorus* (fig. 55).—Abundant in meadows of the subalpine region and occasionally above timberline. The flowers are pale yellow at first, becoming whitish, cup-shaped, and from 1 to 2 inches broad. This plant resembles the narcissus anemone in general appearance, from which it may be distinguished by the smoothness of its foliage and by the fact that the numerous pistils develop into a cluster of small pods, each containing several seeds. The leaves are palmately five- to seven-parted, the divisions toothed.

Buttercups are usually easy to recognize because of their shiny yellow petals that often appear as though varnished and their usually much-dissected leaves. They are sometimes confused with the cinquefoils, a group of the rose family having five-petaled yellow flowers. These two groups may be distinguished by a glance at the calyx. The calyx of the buttercups is made up of five separate green or yellowish sepals, while the sepals of the cinquefoils are united into a saucer-shaped calyx having five main divisions and five alternating bractlets. The name of this genus, *Ranunculus,* is from an old Greek word meaning "little frog," in reference, probably, to the marshy places in which buttercups are usually found. There are several species of buttercups growing at all altitudes in the park. The following key will help to distinguish the kinds of buttercups most frequently seen:

a. Plants aquatic, floating.
   b. Flowers white, leaves all finely dissected.. **White water crowfoot** (p. 66)
   bb. Flowers yellow, submerged leaves finely dissected....................
                   Yellow water crowfoot (p. 66)
aa. Plants usually not floating, rooted in mud or shallow water.
   b. Plants producing runners or rooting at the nodes.
      c. Leaves all basal, roundish with crenate margins...................
                           Alkali buttercup (p. 66)
      cc. Leaves along the stems.
         d. Leaves long and very narrow, entire.. **Trailing buttercup** (p. 66)
         dd. Leaves lobed or divided.
            e. Leaves three-parted, the segments again
               lobed, plant rough-pubescent.... **Macoun buttercup** (p. 66)
            ee. Leaves palmately three-seven lobed, smooth..............
                          Water crowfoot (p. 66)
   bb. Plants without runners, not rooting at the nodes.
      c. Petals usually more than five.
         d. Leaves simple and entire..... **Caltha-flowered buttercup** (p. 66)
         dd. Leaves thrice compound and dissected into
            many narrow divisions, petioles long.... **Nuttall buttercup** (p. 66)
      cc. Petals usually five.
         d. Leaves of two kinds, basal ones undivided.
            e. Sepals lavender-tinged........ **Sagebrush buttercup** (p. 66)
            ee. Sepals yellow or greenish..... **Heart-leaved buttercup** (p. 66)
         dd. Basal and stem leaves alike.
            e. Foliage and achenes smooth.
              f. Leaves deeply parted into threadlike divisions,
                 often reddish when young...... **Snow buttercup** (p. 66)
              ff. Leaves bright green, lobed and
                 lobes parted again........ **Subalpine buttercup** (p. 66)
            ee. Foliage and achenes usually pubescent...................
                       Birdfoot buttercup (p. 66)

Figure 57. **Snow buttercup, flowers from ½ to 1¼ inches broad.**

Figure 58. **Snow buttercup, one blossom, coming through snow.**

Figure 59. **Columbian rock clematis, flowers 1 - 2 inches long.**

Figure 60. **Bush clematis.**

Figure 62. **Monkshood.**

Figure 61. **Narcissus anemone.**

Shore buttercup, *Ranunculus cymbalaria.*—A plant with simple crenate leaves, spreading by means of stolens similar to strawberry runners that eventually root and start new plants. It grows in moist meadows, especially on alkali or salty soil, and has been found in Horseshoe Park and along Cow Creek (foot of Twin Sisters).

Trailing buttercup or **spearwort,** *Ranunculus flammula* var. *filiformis.*—Found in very wet places around lakes and beaver ponds. Its leaves are entire and very narrow, ⅛-inch or less in width, its stems slender and rooting at the nodes. The variety in the park is more or less hairy.

Nuttall buttercup, *Ranunculus nuttallii.*—A plant with thrice compound leaves, each of the divisions petioled and much dissected. The sepals are yellow and petal-like, the petals very small and sometimes lacking. It is frequently found in spring and early summer on moist, partially shaded hillsides.

Caltha-flowered buttercup, *Ranunculus alismaefolius.*—This plant has entire leaves which are from 1 inch to 2½ inches long and from ¼- to ¾-inch wide. Each flower has five or more oblong petals. This is the only one of the buttercups, besides the trailing buttercup, which has all of the leaves undivided. It is found along streams, lakes, and in other moist places of the subalpine and alpine regions.

Snow buttercup, *Ranunculus adoneus* (figs. 57 and 58).—The most conspicuous and showy of the buttercups. Its large flowers are from ½ to 1¼ inches broad and brilliant yellow, almost poppylike in appearance; its leaves are ternately dissected into narrow divisions. It is found in the upper subalpine and alpine regions, beginning to bloom as soon as the snow melts. The beautiful flowers are often found right at the edge of the snow, and sometimes they even come up through it.

Pygmy buttercup, *Ranunculus pygmaeus.* — A tiny rare plant with slender, weak stems, sometimes found in moist rock crevices and on ledges in the subalpine and alpine regions.

Ranunculus natans, a yellow-flowered species growing in shallow water or on mud, occurs in some of the ponds. **Macoun buttercup,** *Ranunculus macounii,* is a stout plant of wet meadows with elongating stems which root at the nodes. **Sagebrush buttercup,** *Ranunculus glaberrimus,* is a very early blooming plant with comparatively large blossoms. It occurs in the foothills and lower montane areas in the park on both sides of the Continental Divide, sometimes among sagebrush and occasionally under lodgepole pines. The **heart-leaved buttercup,** *Ranunculus cardiophyllus,* is a large flowered species of montane meadows, blooming in early summer.

Subalpine buttercup, *Ranunculus eschscholtzii (Ranunculus alpeophilus),* is found in both the alpine and subalpine zones. At the higher altitudes, it sometimes has extra large flowers, almost an inch across, and is then called var. *eximius.* Other species which occur in the park are the **birdfoot buttercup,** *Ranunculus pedatifidus; Ranunculus acriformis; Ranunculus inamoenus; Ranunculus sceleratus; and Ranunculus abortivus,* an introduced weed.

White water crowfoot, *Ranunculus aquatilis.*—An aquatic plant with white, buttercup-like flowers and finely dissected, floating leaves; found in ponds of the montane zone where it forms large floating masses of brownish green and is quite conspicuous when starred with its white flowers. **Yellow water crowfoot,**

Ranunculus gmelinii, grows with some leaves above the water level and some beneath it.

Clematis.—Mostly trailing, somewhat woody plants with opposite, compound leaves and conspicuous clusters of plumed achenes. The **western virginsbower,** *Clematis ligusticifolia,* with small white flowers in panicles and very conspicuous clusters of feathery fruits, is a common vine of the foothills and has been found near Estes Park village. This seems to be the upper limit of its range.

Columbian rock clematis, *Clematis columbiana* (fig. 59), and the **subalpine clematis,** *Clematis pseudoalpina,* are trailing vines found in the moist woods of the montane and subalpine regions where they bloom in June. The former has three leaflets, entire or somewhat toothed, and the latter, a more delicate plant, has three to seven variously toothed or parted leaflets. Their similar flowers are borne singly, each having four long-pointed blue or purplish sepals 1 to 2 inches long. Later in the season, the plumed seed clusters make them conspicuous.

Bush clematis or **sugar bowls,** *Clematis hirsutissima* (fig. 60). — An erect, pubescent plant with thick, dark purple sepals, found on the lower slopes of Twin Sisters Mountain and in the Grand Lake region.

Meadowrue, *Thalictrum,* is sometimes mistaken for maidenhair fern or columbine as the leaves are similar and the rue does not have conspicuous flowers. In some species, the pistillate and staminate flowers are on different plants. The latter consists of tassels of long slender stamens. The **alpine meadowrue,** *Thalictrum alpinum,* a dwarf plant with perfect flowers, is found in subalpine and alpine meadows. The **few-flowered meadowrue,** *Thalictrum sparsiflorum,* with perfect flowers, and **Fendler meadowrue,** *Thalictrum fendleri,* with dioecious flowers, are both found in moist aspen groves of the montane. The last two may be distinguished, if found together, because Fendler meadowrue is a bluish-green and the few-flowered meadowrue is more yellowish-green in color. **Veiny meadowrue,** *Thalictrum venulosum,* and **western meadowrue,** *Thalictrum occidentale,* also occur.

American pasqueflower, *Pulsatilla ludoviciana (Anemone patens)* (fig. 56).— This plant comes through the ground sometimes as early as March, clothed in fur-covered sepals and involucre. It is one of the most beautiful, conspicuous of the early spring flowers. The large lavender blossoms with their gold centers resemble the garden crocus, to which this plant is in no way related. With the advancing spring, it follows the disappearance of the snow up the mountain slopes all the way from the foothills to the alpine, blooming in clumps among the rocks or on the open grassland. Each of the many achenes has a long plumed style. As they ripen, these styles lengthen, giving the seed cluster a feathery appearance and providing a sail for each individual seed so that it can be carried long distances by the wind.

Narcissus anemone, *Anemone narcissiflora* (fig. 61).—A hairy plant of the subalpine and alpine meadows with three or more (rarely one) white flowers subtended by a sessile involucre. When the sepals fall, a broad head of smooth black achenes is left.

Meadow anemone, *Anemone canadensis.*—A hairy plant of moist aspen groves and streambanks found in the montane zone and lower, with forking stems each bearing a single white flower subtended by a sessile involucre. The white sepals are satiny-hairy on the outside.

Windflower or **Pacific anemone,** *Anemone multifida* var. *globosa.*—A slender plant with solitary long-peduncled red, white, or yellowish flowers. Stem, leaves, and sepals hairy; achenes densely woolly. Found occasionally on hillsides of the montane and subalpine zones. **Thimbleweed,** *Anemone cylindrica,* a white-flowered species in which the receptacle elongates so that the heads of woolly achenes suggest thimbles, occurs along the eastern side of the park. **Northern anemone,** *Anemone parviflora,* rare in this area, has been collected at Thunder Pass.

Colorado blue columbine, *Aquilegia caerulea* (fig. 63).—The State flower of Colorado. A beautiful plant with flowers 2 to 3 inches across of blue and white with very long slender spurs is found throughout the park. Originally abundant in the Rocky Mountains, this plant has become scarce through thoughtless picking and digging. This vandalism is now prohibited by law in the State of Colorado. In the park, where these plants have been protected for several years, they may be found abundantly in subalpine areas, especially on rockslides, where they seem to thrive particularly well. The color of the blossoms on the plants found at high altitudes is often pale and sometimes even white. In shady, moist situations, such as montane aspen groves and ravines, flowers of rich deep blue will be found. A spurless variety of this plant, the **star-flowered columbine,** *Aquilegia caerulea daileyae,* was named from plants found in the Estes Park region.

Dwarf blue columbine or **Rocky Mountain columbine,** *Aquilegia saximontana* (fig. 64).—A rare dwarf plant only a few inches high with blue flowers having short, curved spurs, grows where sheltered by large rocks of the alpine region.

Rocky Mountain red columbine, *Aquilegia elegantula* (fig. 66). — A plant with red and yellow flowers is found in moist places on the western slope, mainly in montane forests.

Larkspur, *Delphinium.*—Plants with lobed or dissected leaves and spikes of irregular flowers, usually dark blue. The upper sepal is produced into a spur from which the plants take their common name.

Nelson larkspur, *Delphinium nelsonii* (fig. 67).—An early blooming plant from 4 inches to a foot high, with very rich, dark purplish-blue flowers, found on montane hillsides and in the foothills. It blooms in May and early June.

Mountain larkspur, *Delphinium ramosum.*—A tall plant 3 to 7 feet high, found in aspen groves of the montane zone, blooms in August. Its spike becomes elongated in fruit, sometimes with a few slender branches. Pods pubescent. **Western larkspur,** *Delphinium occidentale* var. *cucullatum,* has been collected near the western border of the park.

Subalpine larkspur, *Delphinium barbeyi.*—A tall plant 2 to 4 feet high, growing in dense clumps in moist situations of the subalpine region, with short, crowded spikes of very deep blue flowers. Inflorescence often branched.

Monkshood, *Aconitum.*—Tall plants similar to the larkspur but with upper sepal forming a helmet instead of a spur and either blue or white flowers. These plants are considered to be poisonous. **American monkshood,** *Aconitum columbianum,* with a long loose raceme of blue or whitish flowers, occurs on moist ground of the montane and subalpine regions. (See fig. 62.)

Figure 63. **Colorado blue columbine.**

Figure 64. **Dwarf blue columbine.**

Figure 65. **Baneberry.**

Figure 66. **Rocky Mountain red columbine.**

Figure 67. **Nelson larkspur.**

69

Baneberry, *Actaea.*—Plants of moist thickets with compound leaves and spikes of showy red or white berries, which should not be eaten. *Actaea rubra* (fig. 65) is found in moist aspen thickets, especially along the lower part of the Fern Lake Trail and in other similar locations.

BARBERRY FAMILY *(BERBERIDACEAE)*

Plants of this family are shrubs with yellow blossoms and spiny-toothed leaves. Only one species is native in the park.

Creeping hollygrape or **creeping mahonia,** *Mahonia repens (Berberis repens)* (fig. 68).—A dwarf shrub, 6 to 10 inches high, with hollylike leaflets, blooming in May and June, with clusters of yellow blossoms. The blue berries are found in late summer and autumn. They make delicious jelly when combined with apply or some other fruit and are much prized in the Northwest where a related species is abundant and grows much larger. Hollygrape leaves often turn red, dark purple, or yellow in the autumn and winter.

POPPY FAMILY *(PAPAVERACEAE)*

Pricklypoppy, *Argemone polyanthemos (Argemone intermedia),* with large, handsome white flowers having yellow centers and glaucous foliage covered with very sharp, light-colored prickles, is a newcomer to these higher altitudes. Originally a plains species, it has spread during recent years along roadways until now it is quite frequently seen within the park.

Alpine poppy, *Papaver nudicaule* var. *radicatum,* has been found in rockslides on a few high peaks in the park. It has two sepals covered with black hairs and usually four yellow petals, but a form without petals has been found on Specimen Mountain.

FUMITORY FAMILY *(FUMARIACEAE)*

Plants with irregular flowers having two sepals and finely dissected, usually smooth leaves. The bleedingheart and Dutchman's breeches belong to this family. Only one species has been found in the park.

Golden smoke, *Corydalis aurea* (fig. 69).—A very attractive plant forming clumps of pale or bluish-green feathery foliage. In May and June, short racemes of yellow flowers appear close to the ground. This plant thrives in disturbed soil and is seen frequently along roadsides. It appeared abundantly on the burned area following the Twin Sisters fire in 1929.

MUSTARD FAMILY *(CRUCIFERAE)*

This family receives its scientific name from the characteristic crosslike appearance of its four-petaled flowers. The ovary is above the other flower parts, and the two-valved pod is termed a *silique*. It may vary in shape from almost circular, as in the pennycress, to linear, as in the wallflowers. Most of the plants have a peppery taste. Many garden vegetables, such as radishes, turnips, cabbage, and cress, belong to this family.

(There are very many inconspicuous, weedy plants in this family, most of which are difficult to identify. Only the commonest, attractively flowered ones are included in this key.)

Flowers white or lavender-tinged.
        Plant abundant along edges of subalpine streams,
            blooming in summer; leaves bright green and
            sharply toothed; flowers large, white..............**Brookcress** (p. 71)
        Plant of open fields blooming in early spring
            (or of alpine fields in summer).
                Plant very slender, usually solitary; leaves
                    bluish, flowers white or lavender...................**Arabis** (p. 71)
                Plant low, usually in tufts; flowers white....... **Candytuft** (pp. 71-72)
Flowers yellow or dark brownish-orange, white in
        some tiny alpines.
        Plant gray, hairy, rough, often spreading on the
            ground, pods inflated..........................**Bladderpod** (p. 72)
        Plant erect, the alpine ones often very tiny
            and dwarf; pod not inflated.
                Pod linear, much more than twice as long
                    as wide, square in cross section.
                        Flowers yellow, large.
                            Plant rough, abundant, and conspicuous on fields
                                and hillsides in early summer.....**Western wallflower** (p. 72)
                            Plant smooth, abundant, and conspicuous on alpine
                                fields and meadows...............**Alpine wallflower** (p. 72)
                        Flowers dark orange or rarely brownish.......................
                                Wheeler wallflower (p. 72)
                Pod rarely more than twice as long as broad, flattened
                    in cross section, often twisted.....................**Draba** (p. 72)

Brookcress, *Cardamine cordifolia.*—A handsome plant frequently found along subalpine streams. It is a foot or more tall with a terminal raceme of white flowers somewhat resembling those of the garden candytuft, and heart-shaped leaves with toothed margins. **Bittercress,** *Cardamine pennsylvanica,* is a plant with small white flowers and very leafy stems. The leaves are compound of small entire or toothed leaflets. This has been found along the Thunder Pass Trail in the Never Summer Range.

Arabis or **rockcress,** *Arabis.*—Slender, rather inconspicuous plants with small white or lavender flowers and linear pods are very abundant on the montane fields and hillsides, blooming in April, May, and June. **Arabis holboellii** *(Arabis holboellii),* with hairy leaves and stem and pendent pods, is the earliest to bloom. *Arabis drummondii,* with smooth, glaucous foliage, auriculate-clasping stem leaves, and erect pods, and *Arabis hirsuta,* with erect pods and hairy, auriculate stem leaves, are both found in early summer. *Arabis divaricarpa* is also reported for this region. Early in the spring, many of these plants are attacked by a yellow rust, a fungus parasite which grows in the tissue of the arabis plant and in fruiting gives the leaves a yellow color. These little rosettes of yellow leaves, very flowerlike in appearance, are quite conspicuous on the fields and hillsides in April. **Tower mustard,** *Arabis glabra,* an introduced weed on disturbed soil, occurs in the Estes Park area.

Mountain candytuft, *Thlaspi alpestre.*—Tufted plants with wavy-margined, glaucous leaves, headlike racemes of white four-petaled flowers, and triangular or obcordate pods, are common on fields and open slopes of the montane and foothill regions in early spring, blooming in Estes Park in April and May. It also occurs in moist places above timberline in early summer. **Field pennycress,** *Thlaspi arvense,* an introduced weed, is occasionally seen around dwellings.

Fernleaf candytuft, *Smelowskia calycina,* is a tufted alpine plant of rocky slopes and crevices with white or lavender flowers. **Bladderpod,** *Lesquerella montana,* is a rough, grayish plant with stems spreading on the ground and turned up at the tips, bearing terminal raceme of pale yellow flowers. Pods more or less inflated. Frequent on dry, sandy, or stony soil of the montane zone.

Wallflower, *Erysimum.*—Conspicuous plants found throughout the park with yellow, orange, or brown (rarely purplish), four-petaled flowers. The petals are broad above and narrowed into a slender "claw" at the base. The scientific name is from a Greek word meaning to draw blisters and probably refers to the early use of the acrid juice of these plants for that purpose. Even today, the name "blister cress" is sometimes used for them.

Western wallflower, *Erysimum asperum* (fig. 70).—Very common on fields and open slopes of the montane zone and lower. The flowers are orange-yellow, conspicuous in June and early July. There is a form of this with burnt orange or brownish flowers which has been called **Wheeler wallflower.** It is the commonest form in the southeastern area of the park in the upper montane and subalpine regions. **Alpine wallflower,** *Erysimum nivale,* a perennial plant with fragrant lemon-yellow flowers, is found above timberline. This may occasionally have pink or purple blossoms.

Draba or **rockcress.**—Small plants with yellow or white, four-petaled flowers, and flattened, ovate to lanceolate pods. Several are diminutive plants growing at very high altitudes, and some are inconspicuous weeds. The **twisted pod draba,** *Draba streptocarpa* (fig. 71), is the most conspicuous and is frequently found in the park. It has small, somewhat bristly leaves in little rosettes and blooms in May and June in the montane region where it is often found in colonies under ponderosa pine trees. Later in the season, it will be found at high altitudes. Dwarf plants are sometimes seen among rocks on the highest summits. The flower is golden yellow and the pods distinctly twisted, as the specific name implies. A similar yellow-flowered species, which has less twisted pods, is **golden draba,** *Draba aurea. Draba nemorosa* is a slender, annual plant of open ground. Other yellow-flowered species of draba found in the park are: **shiny draba,** *Draba stenoloba;* **yellow draba,** *Draba chrysantha;* **showy draba,** *Draba spectabilis; Draba lutea; Draba crassifolia;* and *Draba crassa.* Rare white-flowered species found in the tundra are *Draba fladnizensis, Draba lanceolata,* and *Draba nivalis.*

The following additional species belonging to this family, most of which are inconspicuous weeds, are found here: **Peppergrass,** *Lepidium apetalum;* **tumble-mustard,** *Sisymbrium altissimum,* and *Sisymbrium officinale;* **tansymustard,** *Sophia hartwegiana,* and *Descurainia sophia;* **cress,** *Rorippa sinuata,* and *Rorippa islandica* var. *hispida;* **thelypody,** *Thelypodium paniculatum;* **shepherds purse,** *Capsella bursa-pastoris,* and *Barbarea orthoceras.*

CAPER FAMILY (*CAPPARIDACEAE*)

This family is characterized by having four petals as is the mustard family, but in the caper family the pod is one-celled and elevated on a slender stalk, and in the one species found in the park the leaves are palmately compound of three entire leaflets.

Rocky Mountain beeplant, *Cleome serrulata.*—A tall plant with conspicuous racemes of reddish-purple, or occasionally white, flowers, the raceme becoming very long in fruit. Occasionally found along roadsides of the montane zone and lower.

Figure 69. **Golden smoke.**

Figure 68. **Creeping hollygrape.**

Figure 71. **Twisted pod draba.**

Figure 70. **Western wallflower.**

Figure 73. **Kings crown.**

Figure 72. **Yellow stonecrop.**

Figure 73a. **Rose crown.**

STONECROP FAMILY *(CRASSULACEAE)*

Rock-loving plants with smooth fleshy leaves adapted for water storage and four or five petals. These plants take their generic name from the Latin verb *sedere,* "to sit," because of their habit of growing on rocks.

Yellow stonecrop, *Sedum lanceolatum* (fig. 72).—A very common plant of stony ground, found from the plains to the alpine. The little rosettes of fleshy leaves appear very early, but the yellow flowers do not open until the middle of June in the montane zone. In August, this plant is found in bloom in the higher altitudes. It frequently grows on rocks or in rock crevices where it thrives with a minimum amount of water.

Rose crown, *Sedum rhodanthum* (fig. 73a).—A beautiful plant with a cluster of rose-pink blossoms found frequently along subalpine streams and occasionally in wet places of all zones.

Kings crown, *Sedum rosea* ssp. *integrifolium* (fig. 73).—A fleshy plant from 2 to 8 inches high with a crowded terminal cluster of very dark red or purplish, dioecious blossoms. It is found in July and later in the alpine and occasionally lower. Late in summer, the entire plant often turns a brilliant red.

SAXIFRAGE FAMILY *(SAXIFRAGACEAE)*

A family including many rock plants and taking its name, that means "rock breaker" in Latin, from the habit of many of its members of growing on or among rocks. Many of the species are arctic or alpine in their distribution.

Flowers yellow or purple.
    Flowers yellow, small plants of alpine zone.
        Plant with runners; leaves hairy or at least ciliate
          on the margins......................**Whiplash saxifrage** (p. 75)
        Plant without runners; leaves smooth in
          tiny rosettes.....................**Yellow alpine saxifrage** (p. 75)
    Flowers purple; plants growing in rock crevices,
        not alpine................................**James saxifrage** (p. 75)
Flowers white or greenish.
    Flowers white, in heads, open panicles, or solitary, never
        in spikes or racemes.
        Stems leafy.
          Petals with small colored dots, basal leaves
            in rosettes.........................**Dotted saxifrage** (p. 75)
          Petals without colored dots; alpine plants of moist
            shaded crevices.
            Plant with bulblets in the axils of the
              leaves........................**Nodding saxifrage** (p. 75)
            Plant without such bulblets, very small and
              delicate, weak-stemmed.....**Weak-stemmed saxifrage** (p. 75)
        Stems not truly leafy, sometimes bearing one leaflike bract.
          Stem with one leaflike bract about the middle;
            petals fringed......................**Fringed parnassia** (p. 77)
          Stems entirely leafless.
          Spring blooming plant of fields, woods, or tundra;
            flowers at first in a dense cluster that
            later elongates....................**Snowball saxifrage** (p. 75)
          Summer blooming plant of subalpine and alpine
            brooksides and wet ground............**Brook saxifrage** (p. 75)

Flowers greenish, in spikelike racemes.
    Racemes many-flowered, crowded; plants often growing
        in rock crevices . . . . **Alumroot** (p. 77)
    Racemes with a few cap-shaped flowers widely spaced,
        plants growing in moist, shady places . . . . **Mitrewort** (p. 77)

Whiplash saxifrage, *Saxifraga flagellaris* (fig. 74).—A small infrequent alpine plant with brilliant yellow flowers and glandular-hairy stem and leaves. It spreads by means of runners, which accounts for its specific and common names. This is strictly an alpine plant and should be looked for among rocks on the high ridges and rocky summits above timberline.

Yellow alpine saxifrage or **goldbloom saxifrage,** *Saxifraga serpyllifolia (Saxifraga chrysantha)* (fig. 75).—A dainty plant of the alpine rockfields with golden yellow flowers. The petals have orange spots, and the yellow seedpod turns red in ripening. This is a smaller plant than the whiplash saxifrage and has none of the hairs or runners of its relative. It often grows in clumps sheltered by a protruding rock and has been found in bloom on the summit of Mount Evans, more than 14,000 feet above sea level.

Dotted saxifrage, *Saxifraga bronchialis* (fig. 76).—A dainty rock plant with a cushionlike habit of growth. Each rosette of pointed leaves sends up a slender stem bearing several flowers. The petals are white and dotted with orange and dark red. Found in dry pine and spruce forests of the montane and subalpine regions and occasionally above timberline. In the lower altitudes, it begins to bloom about the middle of June.

Nodding saxifrage, *Saxifraga cernua.*—A diminutive plant with slender stem and five to seven lobed leaves found under rock ledges and in crevices in moist, shady situations of the alpine zone. The white flowers are nodding, and clusters of red bulblets are borne in some of the leaf axils. A very similar plant with no bulblets, sometimes found in moss in very shady situations, is the **weak-stemmed saxifrage,** *Saxifraga debilis. Saxifraga rivularis,* a tiny rare prostrate plant, grows in the tundra. **Tufted saxifrage,** *Saxifraga caespitosa,* occurs rarely in alpine tundra.

Snowball or **diamondleaf saxifrage,** *Saxifraga rhomboidea* (fig. 77).—A spring blooming plant in the foothills and montane, occurring in summer in the alpine and subalpine regions. In April or May at the lower altitudes in the park on moist hillsides and among aspens, you may find depressed rosettes of pale green ovate leaves. Soon a stout stem is sent up from the center of this rosette, bearing a dense headlike cluster of small white flowers. As the flowers mature, the cluster elongates until a long inflorescence with scattered clusters of flowers or seedpods result.

Brook saxifrage, *Saxifraga odontoloma (Saxifraga arguta).*—A beautiful plant of subalpine brooks, lakesides, and very wet places. It seems to thrive best among rocks in shallow running water where it is easily recognized by its shining, nearly round, coarsely toothed basal leaves which are from 1 to 2½ inches broad. The tall, slender-branched reddish flower stem bears many dainty small white flowers.

James saxifrage, *Telesonix jamesii.*—A plant of rock crevices with kidney-shaped toothed leaves and spikes of purple flowers. The petals have a round blade and long claw. In the park, this occurs in the upper montane, but in some places it is definitely an alpine.

Figure 74. **Whiplash saxifrage, plant 2 - 6 inches tall.**

Figure 75. **Yellow alpine saxifrage, plant 2 - 5 inches tall.**

Figure 76. **Dotted saxifrage, plant 2 - 5 inches tall.**

Figure 77. **Snowball saxifrage, flowering stalks 3 - 8 inches tall.**

Figure 78. **Jamesia, habitat view of shrubs in flower.**

Figure 79. **Jamesia, detail of flowers and leaves.**

Fringed parnassia, *Parnassia fimbriata.*—In the subalpine bogs and wet meadows, you may find an attractive plant growing in clumps with many smooth, kidney-shaped or heart-shaped leaves at the base and slender flower stems. Each stem bears a heart-shaped leaf at about its middle and a dainty white five-petaled flower about ½-inch across. Each petal is fringed toward the base. **Grass of parnassus,** *Parnassia parviflora,* a similar plant but lacking the fringe, has also been found.

Alumroot, *Heuchera bracteata.*—Found in dense mats on rocky ledges, in crevices, and among stones. The dead leaves are more or less persistent and with the prostrate stems form brown mats against which the bright new leaves show up in sharp contrast in spring. The flowers are small, bell-shaped, and greenish, and borne in short, dense spikes. The leaves are sharply toothed. In autumn, some of the leaves turn rose-color or red. The **littleleaf alumroot,** *Heuchera parvifolia,* is frequent on shaded rocky slopes. In this species, the spike elongates, and the flowering stems are often nearly a foot high. The leaves have rounded lobes. Closely related to this is an alpine plant that has been called *Heuchera nivalis.* This occurs in rock crevices.

Mitrewort or **Bishops cap.**—Inconspicuous little plants of moist, rich ground in shaded pine and spruce forests, with basal leaves and slender stems bearing caplike flowers. The **common mitrewort,** *Mitella pentandra,* is frequently seen, and both *Mitella stenopetala* and *Mitella stauropetala* have been found.

Golden saxifrage, *Chrysosplenium tetrandrum.*—A low smooth plant with alternate, tender, succulent leaves, reniform in shape with rounded lobes. The inconspicuous flowers have no petals, the four or five blunt calyx lobes are yellow inside; the stamens are four, or rarely five to eight. This arctic plant has been found in the park on cliffs in dense shade in the subalpine. It is rare in Colorado.

Woodlandstar, *Lithophragma tenella,* grows near Fern Lake. *Lithophragma bulbifera* is rare on exposed rocks in the montane and subalpine.

GOOSEBERRY FAMILY *(GROSSULARIACEAE)*
Shrubs with or without spines, leaves palmately lobed with radiating veins, flowers tubular, and fruit a berry usually crowned with the withered remains of the flower.

Mountain gooseberry, *Ribes inerme.*—A shrub with sharp spines, usually two or three together, and reddish-purple or dull black berries of good quality for jelly and preserves. Found on moist ground of the montane and lower.

Prickly currant, *Ribes lacustre.* — A low shrub with bristly branches and black insipid berries covered with gland-tipped bristles, found in the upper montane and subalpine regions. *Ribes saxosum* and **gooseberry currant,** *Ribes montigenum,*which has reddish, saucer-shaped flowers, are also found.

Squaw currant or **wax currant,** *Ribes cereum* (fig. 80).—One of the commonest shrubs of the ponderosa pine belt and found sometimes up to timberline. Usually forming rounded shrubs or clumps 1 to 3 feet high, the stems rigid and much branched, the leaves roundish, 1½ inches broad or less, crenately lobed, and with a distinctive odor when crushed. The red, insipid berries ripen in summer and are eaten by birds and small animals.

Colorado currant, *Ribes coloradense.* — A rambling shrub of the subalpine zone with lobed, heart-shaped or kidney-shaped leaves and racemes of pinkish or purplish flowers which develop into black currants. **Wolfs currant,** *Ribes wolfii,* has been found.

Golden currant or **clove currant,** *Ribes aureum.* — This fragrant, yellow-flowered currant, which bears good quality fruit, occurs at a low altitude in the park.

HYDRANGEA FAMILY *(HYDRANGEACEAE)*
A family of shrubby plants with opposite leaves and flowers much resembling the saxifrages. **Jamesia** or **waxflower,** *Jamesia americana* (figs. 78 and 79), is the park's only representative. This is a shrub with opposite, distinctly ribbed leaves and clusters of waxy white blossoms. In autumn, the leaves turn beautiful shades of red. This plant is closely related to the saxifrages and has the same habit of growing on rocks and in rock crevices. It is common in rocky places from the foothills to timberline but will be found most abundantly in the montane. Fossils of a closely related species that grew here 35 million years ago are found in Florissant, Colo.

ROSE FAMILY *(ROSACEAE)*
This is a very large family. Many of its members differ widely in appearance. Typically, its flowers have five sepals, five petals, and many pistils and stamens. The sepals are united at least at the base, and often there are five bractlets usually smaller than the sepals and alternating with them. These flowers may have as many as eight petals and as few as five stamens and one pistil. The petals and stamens are inserted on the calyx which may be from flat to deeply cuplike. The leaves are alternate and all have stipules, at least when young.

This family includes many species which produce colorful or edible fruit. The raspberries, apples, and cherries belong to it along with many others. To identify the shrubs of this group, see "Key to Woody Plants," which begins on p. 25.

Flowers white or cream-colored, conspicuous.
    Flowers having eight petals; seeds plumed;
        alpine plants . . . . **Mountain dryad** (p. 79)
    Flowers having five petals . . . . **Wild strawberry** (p. 79)
Flowers yellow or rose-colored; petals five, sometimes inconspicuous.
    Flowers yellow.
        Foliage glaucous, leaflets three, each three-toothed at apex; plant and
          flower inconspicuous; high altitudes . . . . **Sibbaldia** (p. 79)
        Foliage green or silvery with silky hairs, rarely glaucous, if so the
          flowers conspicuous.
            Plants rough to touch, 1 to 3 feet tall, growing on moist ground.
              Inflorescence a spike; fruit burlike . . . . **Agrimony** (p. 79)
              Inflorescence widely branched; fruit a bur covered with hooked
                prickles . . . . **Bur avens** (p. 79)
            Plants not rough to touch; flowers bright yellow.
              Plant with runners; underside of leaves silvery **Silverweed** (p. 81)
              Plant without runners.
                Foliage, or at least upper part of stem and calyx, dark green
                  or purple-tinged; leaves finely dissected; plant abundant on
                  alpine fields . . . . **Alpine avens** (p. 81)

Foliage light green, silvery or glaucous; leaves compound but rarely finely dissected . . . .**Cinquefoil** (p. 81)
Flowers rose-colored; seeds plumed.
Basal leaves finely dissected; stem, upper leaves, and calyx often rose-tinged . . . .**Pink plumes** (p. 81)
Basal leaves irregularly divided, terminal lobe the largest, but not finely dissected; petals and calyx rose or purple. . .**Brook avens** (p. 79)

Mountain dryad, *Dryas octopetala* (figs. 82 and 83). — A charming dwarf creeping shrub of high altitudes that the uninitiated would never guess was a shrub. It often forms large dark green mats on the stony ground above timberline. Its specific name *octopetala* means eight petals, a rather unusual number among flowers. The cream-colored blossoms, 1 inch or more across, are followed by heads of plumed achenes which make the plants conspicuous even after the petals have fallen. This is a typically alpine and arctic plant. It is also found in the White Mountains, Greenland, Alaska, and in arctic and alpine Europe and Asia.

Wild strawberry. — Small plants with five-petaled white flowers and palmately compound leaves of three leaflets, spreading by runners that root and start new plants. Common up to timberline.

Fragaria ovalis is the common strawberry of meadows, aspen groves, and the edges of montane and subalpine forests. Its leaflets are bluish green, especially beneath, and usually have appressed hairs. The achenes are in little pits sunk into the surface of the red, juicy fruit. *Fragaria americana* is less frequently seen. It has brighter green leaflets with spreading hairs and the achenes are less deeply placed. However, this species is rarely found in fruit here. It usually grows on moist soil, often under pines or spruces.

Sibbaldia, *Sibbaldia procumbens.*—A plant with glaucous compound leaves of three leaflets and very small inconspicuous yellow flowers. It resembles a strawberry plant in general appearance, but the tips of each leaflet have two notches. Abundant in the alpine region where snow accumulates, in places covering the ground with its bluish foliage. It is widely distributed over the Northern Hemisphere and wherever found indicates snow-accumulation areas.

Agrimony, *Agrimonia striata.* — A stout, hairy plant 1½ to 2½ feet high with a slender spike of small yellow five-petaled flowers separated by three-parted bracts. The calyx is 10-ribbed, and together with the enclosed seed develops into a top-shaped, rather hard fruit, crowned with numerous prickles that catch in one's clothing. It has been found along streams near Estes Park.

Bur avens or **largeleaf avens,** *Geum macrophyllum.* — A tall plant 1 to 3 feet high, with large lyre-shaped, pinnately divided leaves, the terminal lobe the largest, and a branching inflorescence. The five-petaled yellow flowers develop into round or oval burs covered with hooked prickles. This plant is frequently noticed along streams and on moist ground of the montane and lower subalpine zones. *Geum aleppicum,* a similar but slenderer plant, also occurs.

Brook avens or **water avens,** *Geum rivale.* — A rather rare plant sometimes found along montane streambanks and on marshy ground. Its leaves are similar to the bur avens, but this plant is somewhat smaller and the five petals are reddish or purple.

Figure 80. **Squaw currant, flowers.**

Figure 82. **Mountain dryad, flowers 1 inch broad, 8 petals.**

Figure 83. **Mountain dryad, in fruit.**

Figure 81. **Rocky Mountain thimbleberry, flowers 1 - 3 inches broad.**

Figure 84. **Greenes mountain-ash, in fruit.**

Alpine avens, *Geum rossii* (fig. 86).—This is the most abundant flower found in the alpine tundra. It grows in dense tufts or mats and blooms profusely with bright yellow five-petaled flowers. The stamens are inserted at the mouth of the more or less top-shaped calyx tube. The very dark green or purplish leaves are mostly basal, pinnately divided, and the divisions deeply toothed. In autumn, the foliage turns a dark reddish color.

Pink plumes, *Geum triflorum* (fig. 85).—A rare plant with compound leaves, leaflets deeply incised, having leafy-bracted stems, each stem usually bearing three purplish flowers; styles very long, becoming conspicuously plumose in fruit.

Cinquefoil, *Potentilla.* — A large group containing many similar plants. The flowers are yellow with five petals and are sometimes mistaken for buttercups. The leaves are either pinnately or palmately compound of from three to 21 leaflets. The common name, "cinquefoil," has a French derivation, meaning "five leaf," referring to the leaves of some of the commonest species, which have five fingerlike leaflets. **Silvery cinquefoil,** *Potentilla hippiana,* a pretty plant with almost white foliage (covered with white hairs) and many lemon-yellow flowers, is common on dry fields and hillsides of the montane zone. Its leaves are pinnately compound, with usually five to seven irregularly toothed leaflets. It sometimes grows in large colonies covering the ground.

The **glaucous cinquefoil** or **blueleaf cinquefoil,** *Potentilla diversifolia,* is very common in the subalpine and alpine regions. Its leaves are mostly smooth but bluish and palmately five-foliate, flowers bright yellow, and petals usually notched. **Beauty cinquefoil,** *Potentilla pulcherrima,* with bright yellow flowers, each petal having an orange spot at base, is frequent in meadows and fields below 9,000 feet. It has a pinnately compound leaf. The leaflets are dark green on their upper sides but white with cottony hairs on the lower side. It is frequently found on moist soil of the montane zone. The **singleflower cinquefoil,** *Potentilla nivea,* and *Potentilla ledebouriana,* small, cushion, alpine plants with bright yellow flowers and three-foliate, grayish woolly leaves, are sometimes found among the rocks of the tundra. In the tundra also are *Potentilla concinna* and *Potentilla rubricaulis.* **Silverweed,** *Potentilla anserina,* is a low plant with solitary yellow flowers on long stems and with stems and underside of leaves silvery white. This plant spreads by runners similar to those of the strawberry plant. It is found in the Horseshoe Park meadow and in other wet places of the montane zone. **Leafy cinquefoil,** *Potentilla fissa* (fig. 87), a common plant with large yellow blossoms, about 1 inch across, erect stems, and hairy, pinnate, green leaves. It often grows in rock crevices or among rocks and on burned-over land. It blooms abundantly in June and occasionally later. *Potentilla arguta,* a stout, coarse plant with white petals, is less common.

Shrubby cinquefoil, *Potentilla fruticosa (Pentaphylloides floribunda)* (fig. 88).—A rounded shrub of moist ground, bearing many yellow, rose-like blossoms and leaves of three to seven leaflets, is common from the foothills to the alpine zone but is most beautiful at timberline and just above. Many other species of cinquefoil grow in the park. The following have been identified: *Potentilla pennsylvanica, Potentilla norvegica (Potentilla monspeliensis), Potentilla plattensis, Potentilla quinquifolia, Potentilla rupincola,* and *Potentilla subjuga.*

Mountain spray, *Holodiscus dumosus.* — A shrub with pyramidal clusters of small white flowers and toothed leaves that are silky and light-colored underneath. It is found infrequently in rocky canyons of the montane, commoner in the lower foothills.

Mountain ninebark, *Physocarpus monogynus.* — A small shrub with rather flat-topped clusters of white flowers in June or July; common on hillsides of the montane zone. The sepals turn reddish after the petals have dropped and the pods are densely covered with starlike hairs. The name comes from the shreddy bark.

Antelope-brush, *Purshia tridentata.* — A low, much-branched shrub of the fields, hillsides and open ponderosa pine forests of the montane region having numerous fragrant, dainty pale-yellow blossoms in May and June. The leaves are usually less than 1 inch in length, wedge-shaped, and three-toothed at the apex. This bush often grows close to rocks, and the first branches to bloom in the spring are the ones which are against rock. You may often find bushes with one or two such branches in full bloom while the buds on the others are still tightly closed. That is because the rock reflects heat and also holds heat, thus lengthening the warm period of each day. This is one of the most important deer browse plants, and continuous browsing gives the shrubs their low, spreading form.

Wild rose, *Rosa.* — These are easily recognized, for wild roses are much the same the country over. The five-petaled, pink to red blossoms are exquisitely fragrant. The red fruits, called "hips," are conspicuous in late summer and autumn, and the pinnately compound leaves often turn lovely shades of red as cold weather approaches. The different species of rose are very difficult to distinguish. *Rosa acicularis* and *Rosa woodsii* are found in the park.

Rocky Mountain thimbleberry or **boulder raspberry,** *Rubus deliciosus* (fig. 81). — A common shrub, bearing, in May and June, many large white blossoms 1 to 3 inches across. The blossoms resemble single white roses. It lack the spines characteristic of other raspberries, grows most abundantly and profusely among rocks, and is common in the foothills and montane region. Another thimbleberry having smaller flowers and larger leaves, *Rubus parviflorus,* occurs occasionally at the edge of the park on the west side.

Wild red raspberry, *Rubus idaeus (R. strigosus).* — Especially at home among rockslides of the subalpine, where it is most difficult to gather the delicious fruit, but it is sometimes found in rocky places at lower altitudes. It has prickly stems, compound leaves with usually three or five leaflets, five-petaled white flowers, and juicy red fruit.

The apple relatives form a group of trees and shrubs characterized by having a fleshy fruit formed by the thickening of the calyx tube which encloses the seeds in their carpels. The common apple is the best example.

Serviceberry, *Amelanchier.* — A small tree or low shrub found occasionally on hillsides and along streams below 9,000 feet, with clusters of white flowers in June, and roundish, toothed leaves. The petals are oblong, and the blue or purplish berries are very good to eat, but the birds and worms usually find them first. Both *Amelanchier alnifolia* and *Amelanchier pumila* are found.

Fireberry hawthorn, *Crataegus chrysocarpus.* — A shrub or dwarf tree with stout spines 1 to 2 inches long, toothed leaves, and clusters of white flowers in May or June. The fruits, called "haws," are red when ripe. Not very frequent in the park but has been found on the rocky hills west of Moraine Park and along Mill Creek.

Figure 85. **Pink plumes.**   *Figure 86.* **Alpine avens.**

Figure 87. **Leafy cinquefoil.**   *Figure 88.* **Shrubby cinquefoil.**

Figure 89. **Parry clover.**   *Figure 90.* **Dwarf clover.**

83

Greenes mountain-ash, *Sorbus scopulina* (fig. 84). — A beautiful shrub or tree, with handsome leaves and large clusters of white flowers, replaced later in the season by brilliant orange-red berries. Its pinnately compound leaves are composed of from 11 to 15 sharply serrate, feather-veined leaflets. They turn a brilliant red in autumn. At lower altitudes, this plant grows into a small tree, and one of its European relatives is often planted ornamentally. Its bark resembles that of an apple tree. In the park, it is found occasionally as a shrub in the subalpine zone. There are a few bushes around Bear Lake and some in Prospect Canyon and along Cub Creek.

The cherry group is characterized by having simple, serrate leaves, bitter bark, leaves and seeds, and a fruit called a drupe, consisting of a fleshy or juicy covering over a single hard-shelled seed. The cherries, peaches, plums, and almonds belong to it.

Chokecherry, *Prunus virginiana* var. *melanocarpa.*—A shrub bearing racemes of fragrant white flowers, later replaced by dark red or black cherries *(melanocarpa* means "black-fruited"). Common along streams and on hillsides where it often forms thickets and makes masses of red coloring in autumn. The **bird** or **pincherry,** *Prunus pensylvanica,* a slenderer shrub with a few white flowers in umbellike corymbs and acid red fruit, is occasionally found along streams and on stony hillsides.

PEA FAMILY *(LEGUMINOSAE)*

This is one of the largest and most distinctive of plant families. It is easily recognized by its *papilionaceous* (butterflylike) flowers and beanlike fruits called *legumes.* All the plants whose flowers resemble the sweet pea belong to it. The two lower petals of these flowers are more or less grown together and form what is called the *keel.* Leaves of all leguminous plants native in this region are compound. In economic importance, this family ranks next to the grass family, for may food materials for both men and cattle are derived from it. It also is a soil enricher because the roots of many of its members harbor nitrogen-fixing bacteria, tiny organisms which are able to take free nitrogen from the air and combine it with other substances, thus making it available for plant food.

A. Leaves palmately compound.
    B. Flowers in a close head.
        a. Plants native, growing at high altitudes.
            b. Flowers one to three ....**Dwarf clover** (p. 85)
            bb. Flowers more than three.
                c. Flowers rose-colored, fragrant, margins of
                    leaves minutely toothed ....**Parry clover** (p. 85)
                cc. Flowers yellowish with purple spot;
                    margins of leaves entire ....**Alpine clover** (p. 85)
        aa. Plants introduced, escaped from cultivation.
            b. Flowers rose-red ....**Red clover** (p. 85)
            bb. Flowers white or pinkish ....**White clover** (p. 85)
    BB. Flowers not in close heads but in spikelike racemes.
        a. Flowers ½-inch long or less; pods one or two seeded;
            leaflets three.
            b. Flowers white ....**White sweetclover** (p. 85)
            bb. Flowers yellow ....**Yellow sweetclover** (p. 85)

aa. Flowers larger, conspicuous; pods several seeded.
    b. Flowers yellow; leaflets three . . . . **Golden banner** (p. 85)
    bb. Flowers blue or whitish; leaflets five or more.
        c. Flowers definitely blue . . . . **Mountain lupine** (p. 85)
        cc. Flowers dingy white or pale blue . . . .
                                   Small-flowered lupine (p. 85)
AA. Leaves pinnately compound.

  B. Foliage covered with silky hairs; keel of corolla sharp-pointed.
    a. Flowers bright reddish-purple.

    b. Leaflets two-ranked . . . . **Colorado loco** (p. 86)
    bb. Leaflets three- to four-ranked . . . . **Whorled-leaf loco** (p. 86)
    aa. Flowers white, cream-colored or lavender . . . .
                                   Rocky Mountain loco (p. 86)
  BB. Foliage not silky; keel of corolla blunt . . . . **Vetch** (p. 86)

Clover, *Trifolium.*—The native clovers are small plants of the alpine and sub-alpine zones with three-foliate, compound leaves and small flowers in heads. **Parry clover,** *Trifolium parryi* (fig. 89), with very fragrant flowers, grows as a ground cover in open spruce forests and sometimes above timberline. **Alpine clover,** *Trifolium dasyphyllum,* is very common among the rocks above timber-line, where it forms mats. It is occasionally found in the subalpine zone also. Its leaflets are narrow and sharp-pointed, almost spine-tipped. The flowers are yellowish, each with a purple spot. **Dwarf clover,** *Trifolium nanum* (fig. 90), a caespitose plant of high mountain summits, with heads containing only one to three rose-colored flowers and toothed leaflets, has also been found. **Rydberg clover,** *Trifolium rydbergii,* with pale flowers, grows under trees and in meadows on the western slope. It may be recognized by the deflexed flowers on the old heads. The common **red clover,** *Trifolium pratense;* **white clover,** *Trifolium repens;* and the **white** and **yellow sweetclover,** *Melilotus alba,* and *Melilotus of-ficinalis,* have been introduced into this region and are found along roadsides and around buildings.

Golden banner or **golden pea,** *Thermopsis divaricarpa* (figs. 91 and 91a).—A very common plant a foot or more high, of open woods, meadows, and hillsides, with erect racemes of bright yellow flowers and three-foliate leaves. It is a con-spicuous feature of the landscape, providing masses of color throughout the foothills and montane zone in June and July.

Mountain lupine, *Lupinus argenteus.*—A plant very similar to the Texas bluebonnet, with racemes of blue flowers and palmately compound leaves of five to nine leaflets. It is frequent in the upper montane and subalpine zones. It is common along the lower part of the Twin Sisters Trail, at edges of lodgepole forests in the Longs Peak region, and elsewhere. The **small-flowered lupine,** *Lupinus parviflorus,* a similar plant with long racemes of dingy-white or bluish flowers, is common on fields around Estes Park.

Stemless lupine, *Lupinus caespitosus.*—Stem very short, flowering spike ex-ceeded by the leaves, flowers small, pale blue. Grows around Grand Lake and in other areas on the western slope.

Wyeth lupine, *Lupinus wyethii* (fig. 95), is a handsome plant which is some-times seen in the vicinity of Shadow Mountain Lake, usually growing among sagebrush.

Colorado loco or **Lambert crazyweed,** *Oxytropis lambertii* (fig. 92).—A showy plant 6 to 10 inches high with racemes of bright reddish-purple flowers and silvery-hairy foliage, common on fields and open montane hillsides. The leaves are pinnately compound of several narrow leaflets. It begins to bloom about the middle of June and is very conspicuous through July. It blooms again, though not so profusely, starting in late August and lasting until hard freezes set in. It has bloomed in the Estes Park region as late as the middle of November.

Rocky Mountain loco, *Oxytropis sericea.*—A plant similar to the Colorado loco but usually taller, 10 to 18 inches high, with many-flowered racemes of whitish or lavender flowers, each with a purple spot on the keel.

Whorled-leaf loco, *Oxytropis splendens,* a very silky-silvery, beautiful plant with purple flowers and verticillate leaflets has been found around Grand Lake. *Oxytropis deflexa* occurs in dry lodgepole forests.

Few-flowered loco, *Oxytropis multiceps* (fig. 93).—A rare, dwarf, early blooming, gray-hairy plant, with two or three purple flowers in each cluster, sometimes found in the montane region. The red calyx becomes inflated after flowering and wholly encloses the short pod.

Vetch or **milkvetch,** *Astragalus.*—A large group of plants with several representatives in the park. Many of them are rather similar and difficult to distinguish. They are separated from the loco plants, *Oxytropis,* by the shape of the keel, which in this group is blunt at the end. The leaves are all pinnately compound. **Limber vetch,** *Astragalus flexuosus,* is a very common plant of the montane fields and hillsides, with spreading stems 6 to 20 inches long, racemes of small pink blossoms, and cylindrical, sometimes curved, pods 1 inch long or less.

Parry vetch, *Astragalus parryi* (fig. 94).—A dwarf, very hairy plant of sandy or rocky soil, appearing early in spring. It may be recognized by its small mats of pinnately compound gray leaves with oblong or roundish leaflets. In June, it bears clusters of white blossoms close to the ground and later, curved pods. Some plants of this genus are poisonous, but a ground squirrel has been seen holding the pods of this species in its paws and busily extracting the unripe seeds, which it ate with apparent impunity. **Mat vetch,** *Astragalus kentrophyta,* is a very low spreading plant with grayish spine-tipped leaflets that occurs on dry banks at the western edge of the park. Other species found here are **alpine vetch,** *Astragalus alpinus,* a circumboreal species, common in the upper montane and subalpine on moist, more or less shaded, banks or meadows, with short racemes of two-toned, pale purple flowers; **field vetch,** *Astragalus decumbens;* **sulphur vetch,** *Astragalus sulphurescens;* **racemose vetch,** *Astragalus racemosus* and *Astragalus miser* var. *oblongifolius.*

Climbing vetch, *Vicia americana,* occurs at lower altitudes and has been collected in the Grand Lake area.

GERANIUM FAMILY *(GERANIACEAE)*

This family has contributed ornamental plants to cultivation and is represented in the park by four native species. These plants have flowers with five petals, usually veined, five pistils united except at their tips, and lobed, toothed leaves.

Fremont geranium, *Geranium fremontii* (fig. 96).—A plant of dry fields and open pine forests, often around rocks, with pink or purplish flowers, the petals usually with darker veins.

Figure 91. **Golden banner, habitat view of plant.**

Figure 91a. **Golden banner, detail of flower.**

Figure 92. **Colorado loco.**

Figure 93. **Few-flowered loco.**

Figure 95. **Wyeth lupine.**

Figure 94. **Parry vetch.**

Richardson geranium, *Geranium richardsonii.*—A taller, slenderer plant with white flowers found frequently in meadows and aspen groves and on other moist ground. Another species, *Geranium nervosum,* has been found along streams of the western slope. It resembles the last in habit and foliage, but it has pink or pale purplish petals with darker veins. **Filaree,** *Erodium cicutarium,* is a common weed on disturbed soil which blooms very early with bright pink flowers.

FLAX FAMILY *(LINACEAE)*

A family of great economic importance in the textile and paint industries. The flowers are regular and symmetrical with five parts in each cycle.

Blue flax or **Lewis flax,** *Linum lewisii* (fig. 97).—A plant with delicate sky-blue flowers about an inch across, borne on the ends of slender stems; common on montane fields and hillsides. This plant was named in honor of Capt. Meriwether Lewis of the Lewis and Clark Expedition.

SPURGE FAMILY *(EUPHORBIACEAE)*

A family of rather curious plants, including several showy ornamental species such as the poinsettia, and some species of *Euphorbia* in which the very small, inconspicuous flowers are surrounded by brightly colored bracts. Most of these plants have a thick milky juice.

Spurge, *Euphorbia robusta.*—A much-branched plant having several stout stems, 1 foot or less in height from a strong root, with milky juice and inconspicuous flowers. It occurs on rocky, sunny montane slopes and fields. The leaves, which wither early and dry up, are alternate and oblong, but above them are numerous opposite, sessile, heart-shaped, or rhomboid bracts. The much-reduced flowers are surrounded by an involucre of green bracts, each involucre containing four crescent-shaped glands. **Thyme-leaved spurge,** *Euphorbia serpyllifolia,* a small-leaved, prostrate plant with milky juice, is sometimes found on waste ground.

WATER STARWORT FAMILY *(CALLITRICHACEAE)*

A family of small aquatic plants with opposite, entire leaves and monoecious flowers reduced to one pistil or one stamen, sometimes accompanied by two bracts. **Water starwort,** *Callitriche palustris,* is frequently seen growing in shallow ponds or in mud in marshy places. When growing in water, it develops two kinds of leaves, broad floating ones and very narrow submersed ones. The little round or obcordate pods are found in the leaf axils. *Callitriche hermaphroditica* is recorded from the western slope.

SUMAC FAMILY *(ANACARDIACEAE)*

A family of shrubs mostly confined to lower altitudes. The **three-leaf sumac** or **squaw bush,** *Rhus trilobata,* with shiny compound leaves of three crenately lobed leaflets and a very distinctive odor, is occasionally found at the eastern edge of the park and on foothills below 8,000 feet. This plant also grows in California where the long slender shoots are much used by Indian women in their basketmaking. They use the sticky red berries that occur in small clusters and have an acid flavor in making a drink similar to lemonade. This plant is not poisonous, but its relative—the **western poison-ivy,** *Toxicodendron radicans*— with leaves of three entire shiny leaflets, each 1 to 4 inches long, occurs very rarely on shady moist montane slopes and more abundantly at lower altitudes.

MAPLE FAMILY *(ACERACEAE)*

A family of beautiful, valuable trees with lobed and toothed (or rarely compound leaves) and sugary sap. The only representative in the park is the **Rocky Mountain maple,** *Acer glabrum,* a several-stemmed shrub, sometimes of large size, usually found growing in rocks in the montane and lower subalpine zones, with gray bark and red winter twigs and buds. It turns a pale yellow in autumn. The commonest form has simple three- to five-lobed leaves, but occasionally shrubs are found which have deeply three-parted leaves or even compound leaves of three separate leaflets.

STAFF TREE FAMILY *(CELASTRACEAE)*

A family of shrubs of which the bittersweet is the best known representative. The only species found in the park is **mountain lover** or **myrtle pachystima,** *Pachystima myrsinites,* a small evergreen shrub with opposite, slightly toothed leaves. It grows abundantly in montane forests on the western slope and possibly may be found in Wild Basin.

BUCKTHORN FAMILY *(RHAMNACEAE)*

A family of shrubs or trees some of which are thorny. The small flowers are in clusters and in the species in the park each petal has a narrow claw.

Mountain balm, *Ceanothus velutinus.*—A low spreading shrub without thorns, with roundish or shiny (as if varnished) oval leaves and feathery panicles of small white flowers. This bush often makes large patches a foot or two high in open woods of the upper montane. It blooms in spring or in early summer, and sometimes a second time in late summer.

Fendler buckthorn, *Ceanothus fendleri.*—A dwarf spiny shrub with entire leaves, silky beneath, and simple terminal racemes of small white flowers; found in the vicinity of Beaver Point and probably elsewhere at lowest altitudes. It usually winter-kills nearly to the ground, thus always looking untidy because of the dead branches.

MALLOW FAMILY *(MALVACEAE)*

Most members of this family are herbs and have gummy juice. The marshmallow of the candymakers was originally made from the juice of one species of mallow. The stamens are united into a column around the pistil.

Modest mallow, *Sidalcea candida.*—A plant bearing a spike of white, thin-petaled flowers, and deeply lobed stem leaves is occasionally found in moist shady places and along streams.

Wild hollyhock, *Sidalcea neomexicana.*—A plant with slender racemes of rose-purple flowers resembling miniature hollyhocks. The basal leaves are roundish with rounded lobes and teeth. This grows on the western slope at lowest altitudes in the park.

Scarlet mallow, *Sphaeralcea coccinea.*—A charming, low-growing, gray-foliaged plant with salmon or tomato-colored, hollyhocklike flowers, common on the plains and foothills, has been found along roads in the park.

Figure 96. **Fremont geranium, flowers about 1 inch across.**

Figure 97. **Blue flax, flowers about 1 inch across.**

Figure 98. **Canada violet.**

Figure 99. **Plains pricklypear.**

Figure 100. **Mountain ball cactus.**

Figure 101. **Stemless evening-primrose.**

90

ST. JOHNSWORT FAMILY *(HYPERICACEAE)*

A family of herbs (in this region) with opposite leaves, the leaves and petals with dark or translucent dots. **Southwestern St. Johnswort,** *Hypericum formosum,* is a smooth plant which is found in wet montane meadows, readily recognized by holding the leaves to the light so that the translucent dots appear. The yellow petals show small black dots.

VIOLET FAMILY *(VIOLACEAE)*

A family of small herbs, with irregular flowers, which are easily recognized because of general familiarity with garden violets.

There are several kinds of violets in the park, but due to the fact that some of them bloom early in the season and most of them are modest in habit, as violets are expected to be, they are not a conspicuous part of the flora, and many people rarely or never see them. The commonest one is the **subalpine blue violet,** *Viola bellidifolia,* which is often abundant on streambanks and moist slopes at the higher elevations. The flower is light blue and the short, leafy stems are often clustered, giving the plant a tufted aspect. Closely related and similar except taller and more spreading is the **Hook violet,** *Viola adunca,* which occurs in moist montane aspen groves or meadows. The **arctic yellow violet** or **twinflower violet,** *Viola biflora,* is a small rare plant found in moss or moist places among rocks on the higher peaks and into the subalpine forest. It grows in all arctic regions of the world. Two related and somewhat similar species are the **Rydberg violet,** *Viola rugulosa,* and the **Canada violet,** *Viola canadensis* (fig. 98). Both have more or less heart-shaped leaves, leafy stems up to a foot tall, and mainly white flowers veined with purple. They often grow together in moist montane and subalpine woods and bloom at the same time, which is usually early summer. The Rydberg violet has larger flowers with the upper petals reddish purple on the back, and the lower leaves are often broader than long. The Canada violet has its upper petals mainly without purple color, and the leaves are usually longer than broad and drawn out into a slender tip.

Swamp white violet, *Viola pallens,* grows on streambanks, often in moss, and in wet meadows. It is a very smooth plant with roundish leaves, and it develops runners after blooming. *Viola renifolia* is similar, but more or less hairy, and does not develop runners. The **meadow violet,** *Viola nephrophylla,* a stemless species with blue or violet blossoms, is found in the montane meadows in early spring.

The **great-spurred violet,** *Viola selkirkii.*—A very rare species in Colorado, occurs as a small colony in a moist spruce forest. The **yellow-flowered violet,** *Viola praemorsa,* somewhat resembling *Viola nuttallii,* has been found in the Never Summer Range.

LOASA FAMILY *(LOASACEAE)*

The plants of this family are covered with rough hairs. They grow along roadsides and on disturbed soil. The flowers have many stamens and five or 10 petals.

Many-flowered evening star, *Mentzelia speciosa (M. multiflora).*—A plant with showy yellow flowers and shiny white stems, opening in late afternoon is very common along the roadsides. The seedpod is cylindrical, an inch or more in length, crowned with the five narrow calyx divisions. **White evening star,** *Mentzelia nuda,* has been collected in this region.

CACTUS FAMILY *(CACTACEAE)*

A family easily recognized by its thickened fleshy stems, covered with tufts of spines. The flowers have many petals and are usually very showy. These plants are well adapted to life in arid regions where most of them grow. They are very abundant in the Southwest.

Mountain ball cactus, *Pediocactus simpsonii (Echinocactus simpsonii)* (fig. 100).—The commonest cactus in this region most aptly described by the name "pincushion." It is globular in shape, somewhat depressed, and covered with stout, radiating spines. In May and early June, it is crowned with pink or rose-colored flowers of numerous satiny petals. It is frequently found on dry open slopes below 9,000 feet.

Plains pricklypear, *Opuntia polyacantha* (fig. 99).—Occasionally found in dry, sunny situations at lowest altitudes in the park, and more abundant lower. The joints of the stem are flattened. The satiny-petaled flowers which appear in June are pale yellow and often 2 or 3 inches broad.

OLEASTER FAMILY *(ELAEAGNACEAE)*

A family of shrubs characterized by berrylike fruits and entire leaves covered, especially on the underside, with scales or starlike hairs. **Bitter buffaloberry,** *Shepherdia canadensis,* is the only representative native to the park. It is a low shrub occasionally found on moist, shaded slopes of the montane zone. The dark green leaves are silvery-scurfy underneath, and the twigs and buds are covered with rust-colored scales. The plant is conspicuous in winter and early spring by the clusters of little, round, rusty flower buds. The pale-yellow flowers open before the leaves appear and are followed in late summer by very bitter orange or red berries.

EVENING-PRIMROSE FAMILY *(ONAGRACEAE)*

A large family of plants characterized by having four petals and an inferior seedpod, that is, the seedpod is placed below the other flower parts instead of being surrounded by them. This should not be confused with the true primrose family (p. 99), which is distinctly different in all respects.

Seeds tipped with a bunch of white hairs.
    Flowers bright purple or magenta, 1 to 2 inches across.
        Inflorescence a spikelike raceme; plant very common along roads and
           burned-over regions..............................**Fireweed** (p. 93)
        Inflorescence axillary; plant rare ......**Broadleaved fireweed** (p. 93)
    Flowers white, pink or bluish, small; plants growing
      on wet ground................................**Willow herb** (p. 93)
Seeds without a bunch of white hairs.
    Flowers tiny, white fading reddish.................**Babysbreath** (p. 93)
    Flowers usually 1 inch broad or more.
        Flowers yellow when fresh, opening in the evening ....
                        Yellow evening-primrose, (p. 95)
        Flowers white when fresh, turning pink with age.
           Flowers 2 inches across or more, fragrant;
              plant stemless ....**Stemless evening-primrose,** (p. 95)
           Flowers less than 2 inches across, opening in the
              morning; plant branched.
                  Leaves finely pinnately dissected ....
                        Cutleaf evening-primrose (p. 95)

Leaves not dissected; stem white and shining ....
Nuttall evening-primrose (p. 95)

Fireweed, *Epilobium angustifolium* (fig. 102). — One of the conspicuous and most interesting plants throughout its long blooming season from early July into September. The brilliant purplish-red or magenta-colored flowers are borne in long graceful spikes. Each individual flower is four-petaled and grows on the tip of the long seedpod. From this characteristic, the genus takes its name *Epilobium,* which comes from the Greek words meaning "upon the pod." The leaves of the commoner form are narrow and pointed, giving the plant its specific name, *angustifolium,* narrow-leaved.

It may be seen anywhere along roadsides, along streams, in meadows, and in aspen groves, but it is most striking and abundant on the burned-over lands, where it is one of the first of the plant pioneers to invade those desolate regions. From that habit, it receives its common name of "fireweed." During the summer, the burned-over hillsides around Bear Lake, on Twin Sisters Mountain, and along the Lawn Lake Trail, as well as many other localities, are brilliant with the blooms of this plant. In the autumn its reddening leaves often add a distinct color note to the scenery. As the pods open, the numerous seeds, each on its tuft of white silky hairs, are carried far and wide by the wind. It occurs in similar locations all around the Northern Hemisphere.

Broadleaved fireweed, *Epilobium latifolium* (fig. 103), has been found along streams on the western slope. This plant is not as tall as the *Epilobium angustifolium* and has fewer but larger and more brilliant flowers and broader leaves. It is a widely distributed species of northern and mountainous regions, known from Greenland, Alaska, and the Himalayas, as well as from all the high ranges of North America.

The **willow herbs** are mostly slender, inconspicuous plants found growing around springs and in moist places. The group as a whole is easily recognized because of the tiny (⅓-inch across) four-petaled flowers of lavender, pink, or white, placed just as those of the fireweed are, on the tip of the long slender pod. But even the experts have trouble distinguishing the species. The leaves are entire or slightly denticulate, the lower usually opposite, the upper ones sometimes alternate. When ripe, the four-sided seedpods split open at the top, the sides curling backward, revealing rows of tiny seeds, each with a tuft *(coma)* of white hairs at the tip. The plant owes its common name, "willow herb," to the appearance of these tufted seeds. Hybrids are frequent in this group so that accurate determination is difficult. The following species have been identified in the park: *Epilobium glandulosum, Epilobium anagallidifolium, Epilobium brevistylum, Epilobium lactiflorum, Epilobium drummondii, Epilobium paniculatum, Epilobium hornemannii, Epilobium ciliatum,* and *Epilobium clavatum. Epilobium halleanum* has been collected in the Never Summer Range.

Babysbreath.—A much-branched plant with narrow leaves, tiny white flowers which turn to red as they wither, and slightly curved, knobby pods; found around buildings and on open fields. The park's two species are *Gayophytum ramosissimum* and *Gayophytum nuttallii.*

Evening-primrose, *Oenothera.*—A group of plants with showy yellow or white flowers, opening either in morning or evening, lasting only a few hours, and turning pink or reddish in age.

Figure 102. **Fireweed.**

Figure 103. **Broadleaved fireweed.**

Figure 105. **Alpine parsley.**

Figure 104. **Mountain parsley.**

Figure 106. **Grays angelica.**

Figure 107. **Swamp pyrola.**

Yellow evening-primrose, *Oenothera strigosa.*—A coarse plant with rather delicate, pale-yellow flowers opening in late afternoon. It grows along roadsides, around buildings, and on old plowed fields. A yellow-flowered stemless evening-primrose, *Oenothera flava,* occurs on disturbed ground on the western slope.

Stemless evening-primrose, *Oenothera caespitosa* (fig. 101). — Occasionally found on sunny, rocky slopes of the montane and lower. This plant grows in tufts among the rocks and bears large white flowers, 2 to 3 inches across, that turn pink with age. The flower has a very long, slender calyx tube at the lower end of which will be found the tapering, ridged pod directly on the crown of the plant.

Cut-leaf evening-primrose, *Oenothera coronopifolia.*—A low plant with pinnately cut leaves, somewhat fernlike in appearance, and white flowers 1 inch or less across. It grows along roadsides and on disturbed ground, blooming in June and July.

Nuttall evening-primrose, *Oenothera nuttallii.*—Flowers similar to the cut-leaf evening- primrose, but the plant is a foot or more high with shining white stems, undivided leaves, and larger flowers. It grows along roadsides.

WATER MILFOIL FAMILY *(HALORAGACEAE)*

Water plants with inconspicuous flowers and narrow, usually whorled, leaves, found growing in ponds or on marshy ground. **Marestail** or **bottle brush,** *Hippuris vulgaris,* and **water milfoil** or **parrotfeather,** *Myriophyllum spicatum* ssp. *exalbescens,* both occur in the park.

GINSENG FAMILY *(ARALIACEAE)*

This is represented in this region by only one species, the **wild-sarsaparilla,** *Aralia nudicaulis,* found occasionally in moist woods of the montane region. The underground stem sends up one or more long petioled compound leaves and one peduncle bearing two to seven umbels of small flowers. Each division of the leaf has, normally, five leaflets.

PARSNIP FAMILY *(UMBELLIFERAE)*

This family is easily recognized but to distinguish the different individual species is a difficult matter. Some of them, the commoner and more conspicuous, can be learned quite easily. The family is characterized, as its Latin name implies, by having the flowers in umbels which are usually compound. It also has hollow stems, and the leaves are mostly compound, or at least very much divided. Flowers are usually white or yellow. Economically, it is an important family, for many vegetables and spices, such as celery, parsley, carrot, parsnip, dill, and caraway, belong to it.

Cow parsnip, *Heracleum lanatum.*—A stout plant 3 to 6 feet high with thick stem, large compound leaves with three broad, lobed leaflets, and enormous umbels, 6 to 12 inches across, of small white flowers. It is commonly seen along streambanks in the montane and subalpine regions. Its name, *Heracleum,* refers to Hercules because of the great size of the plant.

Whiskbroom parsly, *Harbouria trachypleura.*—A plant with umbels of small yellow flowers and leaves several times ternately compound with linear segments. It is very abundant on fields and open slopes, beginning to bloom when barely out of the ground in May and continuing through June when it become 8 to 12 inches high. A very similar plant, **mountain parsley** *Pseudocymopterus montanus* (fig. 104), grows in more shaded areas. The lobes of its leaves are broader and taper at each end.

Alpine parsley, *Oreoxis alpina* (fig. 105).—A dwarf, caespitose plant with yellow flowers, pinnate leaves with narrow segments and very short stem; found among rocks of the alpine tundra.

Angelica, *Angelica ampla.*—A stout plant of streambanks with white flowers in large compound globular umbels, often growing with the cow parsnip and distinguished from it by having the compound leaves three-branched and then twice pinnate with ovate or obovate, finely toothed leaflets. **Grays angelica,** *Angelica grayi* (fig. 106), a stout plant 6 inches to 2 feet high, similar to the *Angelica ampla,* but growing in the subalpine and alpine, with very thick stems and petioles much enlarged and sheathing the stems. It is frequent among rocks at very high altitudes and in thickets at about 10,000 feet.

Other species in this family found in the park are: **lovage,** *ligusticum porteri;* **hemlock-parsley,** *Conioselinum scopulorum;* **sweet cicely,** *Osmorhiza depauperata; Pseudocymopterus sylvaticus;* **sanicle** or **snakeroot,** *Sanicula marilandica;* **cowbane,** *Oxypolis fendleri;* **caraway,** *Carum carvi;* **water hemlock,** *Cicuta douglasii;* and **poison hemlock,** *Conium maculatum.*

DOGWOOD FAMILY *(CORNACEAE)*

A family mostly made up of shrubs, some with very beautiful blooms. Flowers small, in clusters or heads, surrounded by petal-like bracts; leaves opposite. The park's only representative is **red-osier dogwood,** *Cornus stolonifera,* a shrub with dark-red bark occasionally found in the park in moist thickets and along streams, but much more abundant along streams at lower altitudes.

HEATH FAMILY *(ERICACEAE)*

A very large family to which many beautiful ornamental shrubs belong. The corolla is united, or in the pyrolas, of separate petals; the stamens are of the same number or twice as many as the corolla lobes and inserted on the receptacle with the other flower-parts, not on the corolla. The leaves are often evergreen and usually rather thick, never lobed or dissected.

The pyrolas and their relatives constitute a group of small herbs with tough, shiny evergreen leaves, white or pink flowers with five thick apparently separate petals, 10 stamens, and one conspicuous pistil. They are confined to moist coniferous forests and shady bogs. These species, distinguished by the following key, are found in the park: **Star-flowered pyrola** or **woodnymph,** *Moneses uniflora* (figs. 108 and 109); **pipsissewa** or **prince's pine,** *Chimaphila umbellata* (fig. 110); **bog** or **swamp pyrola,** *Pyrola asarifolia* (fig. 107); **one-sided pyrola,** *Pyrola secunda (Rameschia secunda);* **green-flowered pyrola,** *Pyrola virens;* and **least pyrola,** *Pyrola minor.*

Figure 108. **Star-flowered pyrola, plant 2 to 4 inches tall.**

Figure 109. **Star-flowered pyrola, showing flower face.**

Figure 110. **Pipsissewa or prince's pine.**

Figure 111a. **Kinnikinnic berries.**

Figure 111. **Kinnikinnic flowers.**

Figure 112. **Bog laurel.**

Figure 113. **Dwarf blueberry.**

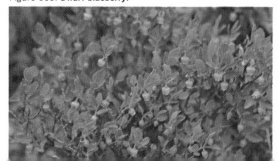

Flower solitary...................................Star-flowered pyrola
Flowers several.
    Flowers in corymb.......................Pipsissewa or prince's pine
    Flowers in a simple raceme.
        Flowers pink.............................Bog or swamp pyrola
        Flowers white or greenish.
            Racemes one-sided.........................One-sided pyrola
            Racemes not one-sided.
                Style long and declined...............Green-flowered pyrola
                Style short, stigma five-rayed..................Least pyrola

The pyrolas are often called by the common name of "wintergreen," but they should not be confused with the aromatic wintergreen of the genus *Gaultheria*. Other members of the family in the park have their petals united into urn-shaped or cup-shaped corollas, and their stems are woody (in *Gaultheria,* very slender and creeping), except in the saprophytic species.

Kinnikinnic or **bearberry,** *Arctostaphylos uva-ursi* (figs. 111 and 111a.) — A charming little evergreen prostrate shrub. It rarely grows more than 6 inches high but spreads out in a green carpet of glossy leaves. The shreddy, reddish bark of its trailing stems, as well as its dainty flowers and berries, suggest its close relationship to the more western manzanitas which belong to the same genus. In May and June, kinnikinnic is covered with waxy, pinkish bells, followed by shiny green berries, which turn scarlet in autumn. These are much relished by the small animals and are called "chipmunk apples" by the children. This plant is one of nature's pioneers, ever advancing on the frontier of poor and rocky ground or following the devastating forest fires.

Creeping wintergreen, *Gaultheria humifusa.* — A creeping evergreen plant growing pressed close to the ground, often in moss, and very inconspicuous except when dotted with its scarlet berries which have a pleasant flavor. It is found in damp places in the subalpine region.

Bog laurel, *Kalmia polifolia* (fig. 112). — This little shrub is one of the loveliest plants of the subalpine region where it grows only a few inches high but blooms profusely in July, with clusters of rose-purple flowers similar in shape to those of the mountain-laurel of the East. The margins of the opposite leaves are in-rolled. It is found along streams, often growing in moss, and around lakeshores.

Blueberries, *Vaccinium.*—Small shrubs with deciduous leaves and small urn-shaped blossoms of white, greenish, or pink, followed by juicy edible berries. They are abundant on the burned-over regions and forests of the subalpine zone.

Myrtleleaf blueberry, *Vaccinium myrtillus.* — A common small shrub with ovate leaves, brownish stems, usually less than a foot high, and large, sweet blue-black berries. **Grouseberry** or **broom huckleberry,** *Vaccinium scoparium,* with green, angled stems, smaller leaves and small red berries, is found with it. The latter, by itself, often forms a continuous green ground cover in Engelmann spruce forests. **Dwarf blueberry,** *Vaccinium caespitosum* (fig. 113), may be distinguished from the grouseberry by its round, rather than angled branches and its very low, more spreading habit. The berries are blue. It is found in abundance in timberline regions.

Pinedrops, *Pterospora andromedea* (fig. 114).—A tall plant with brown, hairy stem, no leaves, and roundish blossoms hanging like bells is sometimes found in the coniferous forest. **Pinesap,** *Monotropa hypopitys,* has been collected in the Kawuneeche Valley.

PRIMROSE FAMILY *(PRIMULACEAE)*

Plants having simple (undivided) leaves and united, five-lobed, regular corollas. The fruit is a capsule, and the seeds are attached to a central placenta.

Flower solitary, rose-colored; plant usually only 2 or
   3 inches high; alpine zone........................**Fairy primrose** (p. 99)
Flowers several in umbels or clusters.
   Flowers in terminal umbels.
      Umbel compound, made up of small umbels.
         Plant common on montane fields,
            inconspicuous...................**Mountain androsace** (p. 99)
         Plant of alpine fields with numerous
            starlike, white flowers................**Alpine androsace** (p. 99)
      Umbel not compound.
         Flowers white with yellow eye, fading pink,
            fragrant; small alpine plant..............**Rockjasmine** (p. 101)
         Flowers pink or rose-purple.
            Petals bent backward; plant of montane
               meadows and streamsides............**Shooting star** (p. 101)
            Petals spreading; very conspicuous plant
               of subalpine and alpine streamsides
               and wet ground....................**Parry primrose** (p. 99)
   Flowers in axillary clusters, yellow...........**Tufted loosestrife** (p. 101)

Fairy primrose or **alpine primrose,** *Primula angustifolia* (fig. 115). — An alpine plant only 2 to 4 inches high with bright rose-purple flowers with yellow eye, usually only one on each stem, but stems sometimes clustered. It is one of the first tundra plants to bloom in late May or early June.

Parry primrose, *Primula parryi* (figs. 116 and 117).—One of the most striking plants of the subalpine and lower alpine regions, growing nearly a foot tall and bearing dense clusters of brilliant rose-purple flowers. The thick, smooth, light green leaves are spatulate oblong or oblanceolate, and all grow in a rosette at the base of the stem. These plants like water and are usually found along the edge of the subalpine and alpine streams or on wet banks from which the snow has recently melted. They bloom in July and August. The odor of the flowers is heavily sweet at first but soon becomes rank.

Alpine androsace, *Androsace subumbellata.*—A small alpine plant with flower stems about 2 inches long from rosettes of basal leaves; inflorescence a compact, compound umbel with numerous tiny starlike white blossoms. It is frequently seen among rocks near Fall River Pass, along the summit of Trail Ridge, and on the high peaks. This is closely related to and may be only·a form of the **mountain androsace,** *Androsace septentrionalis,* which is abundant on montane fields and hillsides but is inconspicuous. The rays of the umbel are longer than the peduncles, and the petals are shorter than the calyx lobes. *Androsace filiformis* is recorded from the Never Summer Range.

Figure 114. **Pinedrops.**

Figure 115. **Fairy primrose, plants 2 - 3 inches tall.**

Figure 117. **Parry primrose, detail of flowers.**

Figure 116. **Parry primrose, habitat view.**

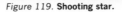

Figure 118. **Rockjasmine, stems about 2 inches tall.**

Figure 119. **Shooting star.**

Rockjasmine, *Androsace chamaejasme ssp. carinata* (fig. 118).—A diminutive, caespitose plant with rosettes of small hairy leaves from each of which a stem 1 or 2 inches high is sent up. This bears a headlike umbel of fragrant white or cream-colored flowers. The eye of each flower is at first yellow but turns pink with age. This plant is sometimes found on rocky alpine slopes, blooming in July.

Shooting star, *Dodecatheon pulchellum* (fig. 119).—This plant is easily recognized by the shape of its flower; the dark-colored, pointed anthers form the apex, and the turned-back corolla lobes give the effect of the "shooting star." It is most abundant in wet montane meadows but has also been seen growing in rock crevices above Chasm Falls, where it was constantly wet with the spray from the falls, and on rocks along the Dream Lake Trail.

Tufted loosestrife, *Lysimachia thyrsiflora.* — A marsh plant with opposite leaves and short, headlike spikes of yellowish, purple-dotted flowers, growing from the axils of the middle pair of leaves. The lower leaves are reduced to scales, the stem not branched. It grows in meadows around Estes Park and is widely distributed across the continent and in Europe and Asia.

GENTIAN FAMILY *(GENTIANACEAE)*

All the members of this family have smooth and opposite or whorled leaves. The corolla lobes of species in the park are four or five, the stamens inserted on the corolla tube. Many of them close the flower except in bright sunshine. These plants bloom mostly in late summer.

A. Corolla saucer-shaped, four- or five-lobed.
    B. Plant 2 to 4 feet high, stout, light green . . . . **Monument plant** (p. 102)
    BB. Plant 18 inches tall or less, slender.
        a. Flowers white . . . .**Marsh felwort** (p. 102)
        aa. Flowers dark blue, sometimes purplish . . . . . .**Star-gentian** (p. 102)
AA. Corolla tubular or funnel-form, its lobes closed or spreading.
    B. Flowers bright blue.
        a. Plants very small, usually less than 4 inches high;
           alpine zone . . . .**Moss gentian** (p. 102)
        aa. Plants taller, usually 6 inches tall or more.
           b. Corolla four-lobed, more or less fringed.
               c. Flower fragrant; plant
                  perennial. . . . .**Fragrant gentian** (p. 102)
               cc. Flower not fragrant; plant
                  annual. . . . .**Rocky Mountain fringed gentian** (p. 102)
           bb. Corolla usually five-lobed, never fringed.
               c. Plants tufted, low and spreading, growing on
                  open, dry fields; flowers
                  usually closed. . . . .**Bigelow gentian** (p. 102)
               cc. Plants taller and erect, usually growing in
                  moist meadows . . . .**Parry gentian** (p. 102)
    BB. Flowers never bright blue, either pale blue, rose-tinged,
        whitish, or greenish.
        a. Flowers several, white or greenish with dark markings;
           alpine zone . . . .**Arctic gentian** (p. 102)
        aa. Flowers not as above; usually with a fringed crown
           in corolla throat.
           b. Flowers solitary.
                c. Flower pale blue or whitish, borne on a slender
                  terminal peduncle; small alpine
                  plant, rare. . . . .**One-flowered gentian** (p. 103)

cc. Flower lavender or
rose-tinged...............**Dwarf rose gentian** (p. 103)
bb. Flowers several to many.
c. Flowers lavender or rose-tinged;
plant slender...................**Rose gentian** (p. 103)
cc. Flowers dingy-white or bluish, very numerous in a
dense, thick, spikelike
inflorescence..................**Marsh gentian** (p. 103)

Monument plant, *Frasera speciosa* (figs. 120 and 121).—A tall stout plant found on open slopes at lower altitudes in the park. The leafy stem is 1 to 4 feet high, the upper part of it densely flowered with saucer-shaped flowers. The four-lobed corolla is greenish with dark spots and bears some fringed appendages.

Star gentian, *Swertia perennis.*—Slender plants of subalpine and alpine marshes with dark bluish or purplish flowers. Corolla saucer-shaped, either four-or five-lobed.

Marsh felwort, *Lomatogonium rotatum* ssp. *tenuifolium (Pleurogyne rotata).* —A slender, rather rare plant of marshy ground with white, saucer-shaped, five-lobed corolla, each lobe with two scales at base.

Moss gentian, *Gentiana prostrata.*—A diminutive plant of the alpine grasslands, also found in moss. Its stem is from 1 to a few inches long, very slender, bearing pairs of tiny, white-margined leaves and a tiny, blue, four- or five-lobed flower which closes immediately on being picked or even touched. The closely related *Gentiana fremontii* has been seen in meadows near Longs Peak and in Horseshoe Park.

Fragrant gentian or **perennial fringed gentian,** *Gentiana barbellata* (fig. 122).—A rare plant, with blue, four-lobed corolla and exquisite fragrance, found in damp woods and sometimes above timberline. The corolla lobes are slightly fringed. A white form is sometimes found.

Rocky Mountain fringed gentian, *Gentiana thermalis (Gentiana elegans)* (fig. 123).—A plant from a few inches to a foot or more in height, usually with a few erect branches, bearing exquisitely brilliant deep-blue flowers; the four corolla lobes are fringed on their margins. These plants are found in sunny places on wet ground of the subalpine zone. A dwarf, one-flowered form of this plant is found at higher altitudes.

Bigelow gentian or **closed field gentian,** *Gentiana bigelovii.*—A tufted plant with clusters of nearly closed blue flowers is found on fields of the montane zone, blooming in August, closely related to the **Rocky Mountain pleated gentian,** *Gentiana affinis,* which is a plant with erect stem usually about a foot high, ovate or oblong leaves in pairs, and clusters of several or many deep blue, funnel-shaped flowers. Found on wet ground in the montane region.

Parry gentian, *Gentiana calycosa* (fig. 124).—A larger plant than the last with one to five goblet-shaped flowers, bright, deep blue when open, blackish when closed. Found in meadows and in a reduced form on stony slopes in the subalpine and alpine regions. If the sun disappears under a cloud, these flowers immediately close up tightly.

Arctic gentian, *Gentiana algida (Gentiana romanzoffiana)* (fig. 125).—The clusters of greenish white flowers spotted or streaked with dark purple identify this plant, which is abundant at and above timberline, blooming in August and September.

One-flowered gentian, *Gentiana tenella.*—A tiny, rare plant with white or pale bluish, four-lobed flowers borne on the end of a comparatively long, slender peduncle rising from a short leafy stem.

Marsh gentian, *Gentiana strictiflora.*—Stem with many erect branches, the plant densely flowered with white or blue-tinged flowers; corolla lobes usually four, sometimes five. Leaves and stem pale green. This is abundant in marshes of the montane zone.

Rose gentian or **amarella,** *Gentiana amarella.*—A plant with small, rose-lilac or lavender, four- or five-pointed flowers, each with a little crown of fringe around the throat. This is a common plant in moist, often shady situations throughout the park. **Dwarf rose gentian,** *Gentiana plebeja* var. *holmii,* is a reduced alpine form with one or only a few flowers.

BUCKBEAN FAMILY *(MENYANTHACEAE)*

Represented in the park by the **buckbean,** *Menyanthes trifoliata,* a plant of cold lakes and bogs, circumpolar in distribution. It is found in some of the subalpine lakes and may be recognized by the cloverlike leaf of three oval leaflets. Its bloom is a headlike spike of small white or pinkish flowers.

DOGBANE FAMILY *(APOCYNACEAE)*

Indian-hemp, *Apocynum androsaemifolium.*—The only member found in the park. It is a branching plant 6 inches to a foot high in this region, with ovate or oblong leaves, dark green and shiny above but pale beneath, and clusters of small pink flowers. The margins of the corolla lobes turn back. The stem is usually light brown or straw-colored, sometimes reddish, and the plant has a milky sap. It is found in sunny, often rocky, locations of the montane region and is conspicuous in autumn because of its yellow coloration.

MILKWEED FAMILY *(ASCLEPIADACEAE)*

Showy milkweed, *Asclepias speciosa,* adventive along roads, is a tall stout plant with opposite, oval or oblong, light green leaves, milky juice, and rose-colored flowers.

PHLOX FAMILY *(POLEMONIACEAE)*

A large family, well represented in this region. It is characterized by its regular 5-merous flowers, that is, calyx, corolla lobes, and stamens, five each. The stamens are attached to the corolla tube. The corolla varies from funnel-form to rotate (wheel-shaped) or salverform (as in the phlox where there is a long, slender tube abruptly spreading at its apex into broad flat lobes). Stigmas three and pod three-celled.

Flowers scarlet or pink, long exserted from the calyx . . **Skyrocket gilia** (p. 105)
Flowers blue, white, or pale yellow.
    Corolla with narrow cylindrical tube and spreading lobes.
        Plants of alpine zone, dwarf and cushionlike, never sticky;
            flowers pale blue or white . . . .**Tufted phlox** (p. 105)
        Plants not as above.
            Leaves simple and entire; flowers inconspicuous;
                calyx papery . . . .**Collomia** (p. 105)
            Leaves lobed or divided, divisions narrow.
                Flowers yellowish, some of the leaves with a few lobes,
                  stem woolly . . . .**Spicate gilia** (p. 105)
                Flowers bluish, leaves pinnatifid, stem sticky
                  but not woolly . . . .**Pinnate-leaved gilia** (p. 105)

Figure 120. **Monument plant.**

Figure 121. **Monument plant, detail of flower**

Figure 122. **Fragrant gentian.**

Figure 123. **Rocky Mountain fringed gentian.**

Figure 125. **Arctic gentian.**

Figure 124. **Parry gentian.**

104

Corolla funnel-form or wheel-shaped.
    Lobes of the corolla shorter than the corolla tube,
      mostly plants of high altitudes.
        Corolla bright blue, anthers orange . . . .**Sky pilot** (p. 105)
        Corolla cream-colored . . . .**Honey polemonium** (p. 105)
    Lobes of the corolla longer than the corolla tube; flowers blue.
      Stems decumbent, clustered plant found abundantly in
        spruce forests . . . .**Subalpine Jacobs ladder** (p. 105)
      Stems erect.
        Slender plant of bogs and wet ground in subalpine
          and montane zones. . . . .**Western Jacobs ladder** (p. 105)
        Stout plant usually much branched, growing on fields
          and meadows, montane. . . . .**Leafy polemonium** (p. 105)

Skyrocket gilia or **fairy trumpet**, *Ipomopsis aggregata.*—A plant 1 to 2 feet high, usually with scarlet flowers. The corolla trumpet-shaped, about an inch long with short, pointed spreading lobes; the leaves pinnately divided into linear divisions. This plant is frequently found on the western slope. Two inconspicuous gilias are found on the east side—*Gilia pinnatifida var. calcarea,* with pinnate leaves and bluish flowers, and Ipomopsis spicata, with pale yellow flowers.

Tufted phlox, *Phlox condensata (Phlox caespitosa)* (fig. 126).—An alpine cushion plant with short leafy stems, opposite leaves, and pale blue or almost white, stemless flowers. The stamens are attached to the corolla tube. In June and early July, the plant is sometimes entirely covered with flowers. *Phlox multiflora,* a taller, less compact plant, occurs in the Grand Lake region.

Collomia, *Collomia linearis.*—A weedy plant with narrow, pointed leaves and small lavender or pink flowers in calyxes, which are thin, dry, and papery at the angles and which enlarge after flowering.

Sky pilot, *Polemonium viscosum* (fig. 127).—An alpine plant with large heads of funnel-shaped brilliant purplish-blue flowers, with bright orange anthers. The long, narrow leaves are pinnately compound, with tiny oval leaflets in clusters along the midrib. This plant is found throughout the alpine tundra, blooming from late June through August. It is well named "sky pilot," for it has been found above 13,000 feet on Longs Peak. *Polemonium grayanum,* with pale blue flowers, is similar to it and is found in similar locations. Both have strong-scented foliage.

Honey polemonium, *Polemonium brandegei.*—This plant has cream-colored flowers but otherwise is very similar to the sky pilot.

Subalpine Jacobs ladder, *Polemonium delicatum* (fig. 128).—One of the most abundant plants found under subalpine spruce forests where it is seen in company with mountain figwort and grouseberry. The flowers are light blue, and the leaves are sometimes mistaken for ferns from the ladderlike arrangement of the numerous oblong or lanceolate leaflets. Its stem is weak and usually branched. The **western Jacobs ladder**, *Polemonium caeruleum,* with erect, slender stem and flowers similar to the subalpine Jacobs ladder, is found in some meadows and swamps. **Leafy polemonium**, *Polemonium foliosissimum,* with similar flowers but stout and much-branched stem, is found at lower altitudes, in meadows, and on roadsides.

WATERLEAF FAMILY *(HYDROPHYLLACEAE)*

Flowers similar in structure to those of the phlox family, but the seedpod is usually two-celled, and the stamens usually exserted, giving the inflorescence a fringed appearance.

Fendler waterleaf, *Hydrophyllum fendleri.*—A plant about a foot high or less, of moist, shady thickets, with leaves pinnately divided into seven to 15 ovate-lanceolate, serrate divisions; flowers white, stamens and pistil protruding.

Scorpion weed, *Phacelia heterophylla.*—Plant hairy with silky or stiff white hairs; stems 6 to 18 inches long, erect or spreading on the ground; leaves lanceolate or oblong, the lower ones sometimes with a few lobes; branches of the inflorescence curving, densely flowered, with white or pale lavender blossoms.

Sticky scorpion weed, *Phacelia glandulosa.*—A stout, homely, sticky weed of roadsides, 6 inches to 2 feet high, with divided leaves and clusters of dense, slightly curved spikes of lavender flowers and ripening pods. This plant is usually very grimy because the dust of the road sticks to it.

Purple fringe, *Phacelia sericea* (fig. 129).—Usually sends up several stems bearing many dense clusters of dark purple flowers, forming a narrowly oblong spikelike inflorescence. The slender stamens protrude from the flowers, giving the spike its "fringed" appearance. The leaves are much dissected and covered with silky hairs, which give them a grayish look. This plant is found throughout the park. In the montane, the flowering stems are often a foot high; in the alpine, only a few inches.

BORAGE FAMILY *(BORAGINACEAE)*

The flowers in this family are similar in structure to those in the phlox family, but the fruit instead of being a seed-filled pod, consists of four seedlike nutlets each in a hard or prickly shell. At the time of flowering, the four young nutlets may be seen at the base of the pistil. The calyx often enlarges after flowering, enclosing them. Often they are edged or covered with prickles that catch in one's clothing or in the fur of animals. The plants thus become widely distributed and are considered pests. The inflorescence of these plants is what is known as a "scorpioid cyme," an elongated one-sided cluster which uncurls as the flowers open, similar to that of heliotrope.

Flowers yellow; seed smooth, white, and shining.
>   Flowers at least ½-inch broad and
>   1 inch long. . . . .**Narrowleaf puccoon** (p. 107)
>   Flowers about ¼-inch broad and
>   1 inch long or less. . . . .**Many-flowered puccoon** (p. 107)
Flowers blue or white.
>   Plant very small, cushionlike; foliage covered with numerous white
>   hairs; flowers brilliant blue; alpine zone . .**Alpine forget-me-not** (p. 107)
>   Plants larger, not cushionlike.
>   Flowers blue; buds often pinkish.
>   Flowers "forget-me-not"-like;
>   seed a small bur. . . . .**Tall stickseed** (p. 107)
>   (p. 109)
>   Flowers bell-shaped or funnel-form . . . .**Chiming bells** (p. 107)
>   Flowers white or very pale blue.
>   Plant erect, stiff-hairy, usually unbranched; flowers white,
>   numerous; seed without prickles . . . .**Miners candle** (p. 109)

> Plants much branched and spreading; weeds growing on
> waste ground; flowers inconspicuous.
>
> Nutlets burlike ....**Stickseed** (p. 107)
> Nutlets smooth and shining ....**Cryptantha** (p. 109)

Narrowleaf puccoon, *Lithospermum incisum* (fig. 130).—The flowers of this plant are light yellow, the corolla has a long, slender tube and spreading lobes; corolla tube about an inch long, spreading part ½- to ¾-inch across; leaves linear and grayish with stiff hairs. A plant of the montane fields blooming in June. After the conspicuous flowers disappear, the plant produces *cleistogamus* flowers, that is, "hidden" flowers which produce good seed without the corolla opening. **Many-flowered puccoon,** *Lithospermum multiflorum,* is similar but has a slightly later blooming season; the flowers are smaller, darker yellow, and more numerous; the plants often form clumps of several wandlike stems; leaves narrowly lanceolate or oblong; fields and open hillsides of the montane zone.

Alpine forget-me-not, *Eritrichium aretioides (Eritrichium argenteum)* (fig. 131).—One of the most charming of the high alpine cushion plants. One of the first alpine plants to bloom. If you should see its patches of brilliant blue among the gray rocks, you will never forget the thrill caused by its beauty. **Forget-me-not,** *Myosotis alpestris,* has been collected in the Never Summer Range and may be expected in the park.

Stickseed.—These plants have pale blue or whitish flowers like forget-me-nots and prickly seeds. Many of them are weeds, and those in the park are all found along roadsides or on waste ground. The following species grow here: **tall stickseed,** *Hackelia floribunda,* is perennial; **western stickseed,** *Lappula redowskii,* is annual.

Chiming bells or **American bluebells.**—These plants are easily recognized by their numerous pendent, bell-shaped blue blossoms. The buds are often pinkish or lavender. The "tube" is the cylindrical part of the corolla below the point where it begins to expand. The species occurring in the park may be distinguished by the following key:

Plants with veiny leaves, stems usually over 1 foot tall, growing on
    streambanks and in wet, shady locations ....**Tall chiming bells** (p. 107)
Plants with leaves usually lacking conspicuous veins except for the
    midrib, usually less than 1 foot tall, of open sunny hillsides or
    alpine situations.
        Anthers included in the corolla tube ....**Alpine chiming bells** (p. 107)
        Anthers extending above the tube.
            Plants of alpine or
            subalpine locations..............**Greenleaf chiming bells** (p. 107)
            Plants of open hillsides of the
            montane zone.................**Lanceleaf chiming bells** (p. 109)

Tall chiming bells, *Mertensia ciliata* (fig. 132).—This plant occurs abundantly along subalpine streams and in meadows, and occasionally at higher or lower elevations. Its leaves are definitely bluish. **Alpine chiming bells,** *Mertensia alpina,* is a rare plant in the park. Its flowers are shorter and more open than the **greenleaf chiming bells,** *Mertensia viridis,* which is the common alpine species. It is frequently found in the tundra and in the timberline region. This plant typically has green leaves, but it is variable and plants with broader, bluish

Figure 126. **Tufted phlox.**

Figure 127. **Sky pilot.**

Figure 129. **Purple fringe.**

Figure 128. **Subalpine Jacobs ladder.**

leaves are common. **Lanceleaf chiming bells** or **field mertensia,** *Mertensia lanceolata,* is the common species of montane and foothill slopes. It is also variable and may have either bluish or green leaves. Some forms have a one-sided leaf arrangement.

Miners candle, *Cryptantha virgata* (figs. 133 and 134).—A plant with very hairy, almost prickly, foliage and clusters of white flowers, like forget-me-nots, close to a stout, erect stem. It is conspicuous on the montane fields and open slopes, blooming in late June and July. If the terminal bud is destroyed, there may be several stems. **Popcorn flower,** *Plagiobothrys scopulorum,* a branched plant with white flowers similar to those of miners candle, has been found on the western slope.

Cryptantha, *Cryptantha flexuosa.*—A plant rather similar in appearance and habit to the stickseeds, but its nutlets are smooth; the whole plant, however, is prickly-hairy.

VERBENA FAMILY *(VERBENACEAE)*

A family with opposite or whorled leaves and usually square stems. The representative in the park is **vervain,** *Vebena bracteata,* a weed found around buildings, with spreading, decumbent stems; foliage rough-hairy, leaves cut and toothed; flowers bluish, inconspicuous in terminal, leafy-bracted spikes.

MINT FAMILY *(LABIATAE)*

This family has flowers with four nutlets clustered at the base of the pistil similar to the last two families and two-lipped corollas, square stems, opposite leaves, whole plant usually aromatic.

Inflorescence axillary.
    Plant aromatic; flowers in whorls in the axils,
        pale pink....................................**Wild mint** (p. 109)
    Plant not aromatic; flowers two at each node,
        bluish-purple..........................**Brittons skullcap** (p. 109)
Inflorescence terminal.
    Flowers in a headlike cluster.
        Flowers conspicuous, bright purplish-rose; plant
            strongly aromatic ....**Horsemint** (p. 110)
        Flowers small, blue or pink; plant not aromatic ..**Dragonhead** (p. 110)
    Flowers in a spikelike inflorescence.
        Stamens equal in length; plant introduced ....**Spearmint** (p. 109)
        Stamens unequal, one pair shorter; flowers often
            clustered; plant native ....**Woundwort** (p. 110)

Wild mint or **Canada mint,** *Mentha arvensis.*—Easily recognized by its aromatic odor. The small pinkish flowers are borne in clusters in the axils of the leaves. **Spearmint,** *Mentha spicata,* has been introduced from Europe into this country and has been found on marshy ground near dwellings in this region.

Brittons skullcap, *Scutellaria brittonii* (fig. 136).—Plant approximately 6 inches high; flowers in the leaf axils, a pair at each node, erect, two-lipped, purplish-blue (or rarely pink), about an inch long; calyx short, with two rounded lips, caplike; leaves oblong or ovate, margins entire; found on open slopes and meadows of the montane zone. **Marsh skullcap,** *Scutellaria galericulata,* a taller plant with finely toothed leaves and smaller blossoms, grows along streams.

Horsemint or **mintleaf beebalm,** *Monarda fistulosa* (fig. 137).—A pungent-smelling plant, 1 to 2 feet tall, growing usually in colonies on moist soil, often in or near aspen groves. Flowers in headlike clusters, purplish-rose, from which the stamens and pistils are exserted. The leaves are pointed and finely toothed.

American dragonhead, *Moldavica parviflora.*—A weedy plant with small flowers in leafy-bracted, terminal spikes found around dwellings and on waste ground. Very abundant on the burned area on Twin Sisters Mountain. Some plants have blue flowers, some pink.

Woundwort, *Stachys palustris.*—Flowers clustered in the axils of the leaves, lavender or purplish, often with darker markings; leaves ovate or triangular, sessile, lower side pale; leaf-margins toothed; plant more or less hairy; found on moist soil.

Prunella or **common selfheal,** *Prunella vulgaris.*—A widely distributed weed found on damp soil around settlements.

POTATO FAMILY *(SOLANACEAE)*

This is a large family, widely distributed in warm regions and includes many plants of economic importance, such as potato, tomato, eggplant, peppers, tobacco, and others. Only two species are found in the park.

Cutleaf nightshade, *Solanum triflorum,* a low, spreading plant of roadsides and waste ground, with pinnately lobed leaves and five-pointed white flowers followed by nodding green berries resembling tiny tomatoes.

Black nightshade, *Solanum americanum.*—Similar to the cutleaf nightshade in habit and flower but the leaves ovate, not lobed, and the berries black.

FIGWORT FAMILY *(SCROPHULARIACEAE)*

This is a very large family, which includes many of the park's most showy and beautiful flowers, though some are inconspicuous. It is characterized by having the parts of both the calyx and the corolla united and at least the corolla irregular, usually more or less five-lobed, but the lobes arranged so as to form two lips. The leaves may be either opposite or alternate, entire, toothed, or pinnately divided. The united, irregular corolla is the best characteristic to rely upon in identifying members of this family. The only other group having this same character is the mint family (p. 109), and in addition to the irregular united corollas, the mints are characterized in fruit by four tiny nutlets, while the fruit of the figworts is a two-celled capsule. The foxgloves, snapdragons, and penstemons of the gardens and greenhouses belong to this group.

Leaves alternate or mostly basal.
    Stamens five; flowers yellow; plant 2 to 6
      feet tall, densely woolly...........................**Mullein** (p. 117)
    Stamens four or two; plant usually not densely woolly.
      Stamens four; stems leafy.
        Leaves fernlike; corolla usually with prolonged beak; bracts
          often present but never brightly colored ......**Lousewort** (p. 117)
        Leaves never fernlike; flowers in dense spikes or heads often
          interspersed with bright-colored bracts.

Bracts brightly colored or white, more conspicuous
than the flowers . . . .**Paintbrush** (p. 113)
Bracts green or greenish, less conspicuous than
the bright yellow flowers . . . . .**Gold-tongue owl clover** (p. 116)
Stamens two; leaves mostly basal . . . . **Kittentail** (p. 117)
Leaves mostly opposite, the lower ones always so.
Calyx five-parted; anther bearing stamens four, the fifth
stamen sterile, often much reduced.
Sterile stamen as long as or longer than the others, either smooth
or bearded; corolla blue or purple,
rarely whitish . . . .**Penstemon** (p. 111)
Sterile stamen shorter than the others, sometimes
reduced to a small scale.
Plant a tall stout weed with inconspicuous greenish or
brownish flowers . . . .**Western figwort** (p. 117)
Plant 8 inches tall or less.
Flowers cream-colored, in a short, dense, one-sided spike;
alpine zone . . . .**Snowlover** (p. 115)
Flowers not as above.
Flowers bright yellow . . . .**Yellow monkeyflower** (p. 115)
Flowers blue or blue and white . . . . .**Blue-eyed mary** (p. 115)
Calyx and corolla four-parted; stamens two; flowers blue.
Flowers in a terminal cluster; stem erect . . . .**Veronica** (p. 117)
Flowers axillary; stem trailing . . . .**American speedwell** (p. 117)

The **penstemons** are easy to recognize by their showy, usually blue or purple
flowers growing in spikelike racemes, or narrow panicles, on unbranched stems.
The opposite leaves are usually sessile. The petals are joined into a lobed, somewhat two-lipped funnel-form or bell-shaped corolla. The five stamens which
give this group its name are inserted on the inside of the corolla tube. One of
these stamens is sterile, that is, it bears no anther but instead is usually flattened at the tip and often bearded. From the latter characteristic is derived the
name "beardtongue," often applied to many members of this group.

Flowers blue or purple.
Sterile stamen smooth; flowers blue
with purple throats . . . .**Tall one-side penstemon** (p. 113)
Sterile stamen bearded.
Leaves pale, smooth and bluish, tapering;
flowers purple . . . .**Purple beardtongue** (p. 113)
Leaves decidedly green.
Blossoms large, ¾- to 1-inch long and ½-inch or more
across, bright blue . . . .**Mountain beardtongue** (p. 113)
Blossoms smaller, ½-inch or less in length, about ¼-inch
across, dark blue.
Plants tufted; flowers scattered or continuous along
the stem . . . .**Low penstemon** (p. 113)
Plant not usually tufted; flowers crowded in heads
or in clusters along the stem . . .**Clustered penstemon** (p. 113)
Flowers dark reddish-purple or whitish; subalpine or
alpine zones . . . .**Dark penstemon** (p. 113)

Figure 130. **Narrowleaf puccoon.**

Figure 131. **Alpine forget-me-not.**

Figure 132. **Tall chiming bells.**

Figure 133. **Miners candle.**

Figure 135. **Broomrape.**

Figure 134. **Miners candle, detail of flowers.**

Tall oneside penstemon, *Penstemon unilateralis* (fig. 138).—Abundant on fields and along roadsides between elevations of 7,000 and 8,500 feet; usually a foot or more tall, flowers purplish-blue; the park's most conspicuous species, blooming in July. So abundant in some seasons that whole fields are blue with it.

Purple beardtongue or **sidebells penstemon,** *Penstemon secundiflorus.*—On fields and hillsides of the montane zone in late June and early July, occurring with the tall oneside penstemon but not nearly so frequent; the purple color and pale glaucous foliage distinguish it.

Mountain beardtongue, *Penstemon alpinus.*—On open slopes of the montane zone and along roadsides. The stems are stout, from 6 inches to 1 foot high, often several forming a clump. The brilliant azure-blue flowers occur in a crowded spike.

Low penstemon, *Penstemon virens* (fig. 139).—Abundant on rocks and in rocky places of the montane and subalpine zones; stems usually several to many; flowers dark blue, small; inflorescence hairy and sometimes slightly sticky. Blooms in June in the montane, a little later higher up. *Penstemon harbourii* is a very rare, matted, creeping plant with purple flowers which has been found in the Never Summer Range.

Clustered penstemon, *Penstemon procerus.*—Occasional in the subalpine, has been found around Bear Lake, in Glacier Gorge, and in the Kawuneeche Valley. The flowers are dark blue, from ⅓- to ½-inch long, in compact heads or verticels; the lower lip as well as the sterile stamen bearded; plant smooth; blooms in August. **Large clustered penstemon,** *Penstemon rydbergii,* is similar to the clustered penstemon, but stem and inflorescence downy, and whole plant is considerably larger. Flowers ½- to ¾-inch long; lower lip bearded within.

Dark penstemon, *Penstemon whippleanus* (fig. 140).—Frequent in the subalpine and timberline region; the very dark reddish-purple color of the flowers distinguishes it. The corolla has some long dark hairs on the inside. One form of this has dingy white flowers.

Indian paintbrush, *Castilleja.*—A group of very showy, beautiful plants, abundant in this region. They do not depend on their flowers, which are rather inconspicuous, for their beauty, but on numerous brightly colored bracts or leaves, crowded at the ends of the stems and among which the flowers are found. Many of these plants are partly parasitic and grow attached to the roots of sagebrush or some other plant.

Floral bracts red, rose-colored, purple, or pink.
    Stem branched, flower-spike red.
        Plant of montane zone and lower on dry hillsides, often with
           sagebrush; leaves narrow;
           flower-spike scarlet . . . . **Narrow-leaved paintbrush** (p. 115)
        Plant of the upper montane and subalpine zones in moist
           situations; leaves broader;
           flower-spike scarlet . . . . **Scarlet paintbrush** (p. 115)
    Stem not branched; plant of subalpine and alpine meadows;
        bracts pink to rose-purple . . . . **Rosy paintbrush** (p. 115)
Floral bracts white, yellow, or brownish.
    Dwarf plant, 1 to 4 inches high, of exposed alpine fields; bracts
        brownish or yellowish . . . . **Short-flowered paintbrush** (p. 115)

Figure 136. **Brittons skullcap.**

Figure 137. **Horsemint.**

Figure 139. **Low penstemon.**

Figure 141. **Rosy paintbrush.**

Figure 138. **Tall oneside penstemon.**

Figure 140. **Dark penstemon.**

114

Taller plants; bracts white, greenish, or yellow.
  Bracts white or greenish; montane meadows;
    stem often branched . . . .**Northern paintbrush** (p. 115)
  Bracts yellow; subalpine and alpine meadows;
    stem never branched . . . .**Western yellow paintbrush** (p. 115)

Three red-flowered species are found in the park. The commonest one, on dry slopes of the montane zone often growing with sagebrush or mountain sage, is the **narrow-leaved** or **Wyoming paintbrush,** *Castilleja linariaefolia.* The corolla is usually green and protrudes from the red calyx and bracts; leaves narrow. Another species with broader leaves, found on moist ground of the subalpine zone, is the **rosy paintbrush,** *Castilleja rhexifolia* (fig. 141). The **scarlet paintbrush,** *Castilleja miniata,* with red-tipped bracts, is found on moist ground of the montane and subalpine region.

Western yellow paintbrush, *Castilleja occidentalis.* —The common yellow-flowered species of the subalpine and alpine zones. The stems are unbranched 6 to 12 inches high and often grow in large clumps. Plants similar in growth and habit to this, but with bracts an calyxes varying in color through all shades of rose to bright purple, are considered to be of hybrid origin.

Northern paintbrush, *Castilleja sulphurea (Castilleja septentrionalis).*—This is the common white or yellowish species found in meadows and on moist ground of the montane zone. The stems are often branched.

Short-flowered paintbrush, *Castilleja puberula.*—A very small plant with stems only a few inches long and brownish or yellowish bracts found in stony, exposed situations of the alpine tundra. The bracts and calyx are covered with long hairs; the stems and leaves are often curved.

Snowlover, *Chionophila jamesii.*—A small alpine plant with a short, dense, more or less one-sided spike of cream-colored two-lipped flowers and a tuft of basal leaves. It blooms in July and early August on the high alpine ridges.

Blue-eyed mary, *Collinsia parviflora.*—A small plant, with opposite leaves and small blue flowers in the axils. Its dark purplish or reddish stems and leaves may be seen on open slopes and montane fields early in spring.

Yellow monkeyflower, *Mimulus guttatus.*—Occasionally found on wet ground and along streams of the subalpine zone. The yellow flowers, about 1 inch long, are borne on slender pedicels; the distinctly two-lipped corolla sometimes has dark spots. The leaves are opposite; the stems weak and often rooting at the nodes. A monkeyflower having a very interesting type of vegetative reproduction has been found in seepage areas of the subalpine zone and described as a new species by Dr. W. A. Weber, University of Colorado. *Mimulus gemmiparus* develops buds inside its petioles. After the leaf withers they are released and may form new plants. This was first discovered by Ruth Ashton Nelson and is not known to occur outside of the Rocky Mountain National Park.
(see MADROÑO, Vol. 21, No. 6, April 1972)

Many-flowered monkeyflower, *Mimulus floribundus.*—A sticky, spreading plant; has been found along banks in the montane region.

Little red mimulus, *Mimulus rubellus,* a tiny annual 1 to 2 inches high with yellow or reddish flowers, grows in seep areas on rocks.

Gold-tongue owlclover, *Orthocarpus luteus.*—An erect plant, 6 to 12 inches tall, with a dense spike of yellow flowers interspersed with green bracts; very common on fields in the montane, blooming in middle and late July. The typical form is unbranched, but due to grazing or some other cause which destroys the terminal bud, much-branched plants are common.

Lousewort or **pedicularis.**—This genus is well represented in the park by seven species. It is easily recognized by the alternate or mostly basal fernlike leaves of the majority of its members and by its spikes of irregular flowers. The corolla is two-lipped, the upper lip hooded and sometimes extended into a beak.

Leaves undivided.
    Flowers purple; plant of montane meadows . . . . . **Purple lousewort** (p. 116)
    Flowers white; plant of montane and subalpine forests;
       foliage often reddish . . . . **Mountain figwort** (p. 116)
Leaves finely, pinnately divided, appearing fernlike.
    Flowers rose-colored or purple.
       Flowers with a long, slender, upcurved beak, resembling
         elephant heads, plants abundant
         in wet meadows . . . . **Elephantella** (p. 116)
       Flowers without a slender, upcurved beak;
         very rare alpine plants . . . . **Alpine pedicularis** (p. 117)
    Flowers greenish or yellowish.
       Plants of montane and subalpine woods; leaves bright green.
         Flowers greenish; plant 2 to 4 feet high . . . . **Giant lousewort** (p. 116)
         Flowers yellow; plant 8 inches to
           2 feet high . . . . **Bracted lousewort** (p. 116)
       Plants of alpine grassland; flowers white or
         cream-colored . . . . **Parry lousewort** (p. 117)

Purple lousewort, *Pedicularis crenulata.*—A plant of mountain meadows with short dense spikes of purple flowers and narrowly oblong, crenate leaves; not very abundant in this region.

Mountain figwort, *Pedicularis racemosa.*—A plant with one to several, more or less decumbent stems, each terminated by a spike of white or cream-colored flowers. The leaves are narrowly lanceolate and minutely toothed. The stems and leaves are often reddish in color. This plant is very frequently seen on moderately dry soil under pine and spruce forests in the subalpine region.

Elephantella or **little red elephant,** *Pedicularis groenlandica* (fig. 143).—The most conspicuous member of this group, with its reddish-purple flowers simulating elephant heads. It is abundant on marshy ground in the upper montane and subalpine regions, blooming in the lower parts of its range in early June and at higher altitudes in July and August.

Bracted lousewort, *Pedicularis bracteosa* var. *paysoniana* (fig. 144).—A tall, erect plant, usually with a single stem and a rosette of large, fernlike leaves at the base, also a few on the lower part of the stem; bears a dense spike of yellowish flowers interspersed with bracts; grows in moist forests below 10,500 feet. The **giant lousewort** or **Grays pedicularis,** *Pedicularis grayi,* which resembles the bracted lousewort, but is much larger and has greenish flowers streaked with red, is sometimes seen.

Parry lousewort, *Pedicularis parryi* (fig. 145), a species with cream-colored flowers and leaves with comblike divisions (similar to those of elephantella), is found at high altitudes and occasionally in a taller form, in subalpine meadows. It is usually less than a foot in height, often only a few inches. A rare species, the **alpine pedicularis,** *Pedicularis sudetica* ssp. *scopulorum* (fig. 146), with rose-purple flowers, is found in the tundra.

Kittentail, *Besseya plantaginea.*—A plant usually having several erect stems bearing dense spikes of lavender or pinkish flowers, from a rosette of oblong, or ovate, thick basal leaves. There are numerous sessile, oblong, or round bracts along the stem. These bracts and the leaves are at first woolly but become smooth with age. This plant is commonly seen in bloom on the hillsides around Estes Park in June.

Alpine kittentail, *Besseya alpina* (fig. 147).—A similar but smaller plant than the *Besseya plantaginea,* with bluish-purple flowers from which the stamens protrude, is frequently found among rocks in the alpine zone in late June.

Mullein, *Verbascum thapsus.*—A tall plant, 2 to 6 feet high, of roadsides and waste ground, usually with unbranched stems but sometimes with a few erect branches. It has densely woolly leaves and long, dense spikes of small yellow flowers. It is not native in this country but has been introduced.

Western or **lanceleaf figwort,** *Scrophularia lanceolata.*—A stout plant with opposite leaves and small greenish or chocolate-colored flowers; corolla five-lobed, the lower lobe bent down; anther bearing stamens four; occasionally found in the montane region.

Veronica or **speedwell,** *Veronica wormskjoldii.*—A small plant with a terminal spike or cluster of small blue flowers, bluish-green pods notched at the top, and opposite leaves; found in wet places of the alpine and subalpine regions. The corolla is four-lobed with nearly equal lobes.

American speedwell, *Veronica americana.*—A plant with axillary racemes of small blue or whitish flowers, opposite leaves, and weak stems which are often somewhat trailing; grows along brooks and in shallow water of the montane zone. The **annual veronica,** *Veronica peregrina,* a small erect plant with tiny axillary, white flowers, followed by rounded, somewhat notched pods, is occasionally seen on wet ground.

Butter-and-eggs, *Linaria vulgaris,* a European plant introduced and widely distributed in America, occurs along roadsides around Estes Park and Grand Lake.

BLADDERWORT FAMILY *(LENTIBULARIACEAE)*

Common bladderwort, *Utricularia vulgaris,* is found in shallow montane and subalpine ponds. It is characterized by whorled filamentous leaves and bladders that catch insects. The flowers are yellow and like those of *Mimulus.*

BROOMRAPE FAMILY *(OROBANCHACEAE)*

A family of parasites growing on the roots of other plants. The park's common representative is **broomrape,** *Orobanche fasciculata* (fig. 135), a hairy, brown plant with no green leaves and with two to several parallel stems, each bearing a brownish-pink flower with two-lipped, five-lobed corolla. *Orobanche uniflora* is sometimes seen.

Figure 142. **Yellow monkeyflower.**

Figure 145. **Parry lousewort.**

Figure 146. **Alpine pedicularis.**

Figure 143. **Elephantella.**

Figure 144. **Bracted lousewort.**

PLANTAIN FAMILY *(PLANTAGINACEAE)*

A family of inconspicuous plants, usually considered weeds, with ribbed, basal leaves and spikes of inconspicuous, 4-merous flowers. The seedpods of these flowers are small, pointed capsules which, when they are ripe and ready to shed their seeds, split in a ring around the middle or below, so that the top comes off like a little elf's cap. The most frequent species is the **common plantain,** *Plantago major,* with roundish or heart-shaped leaves, a cosmopolitan plant found around buildings and settlements. **Tweedy plantain,** *Plantago tweedyi,* with lanceolate, or long, narrow leaves, is native in the subalpine zone.

MADDER FAMILY *(RUBIACEAE)*

The park's plants of this family are rough-hairy and have square stems, small white flowers, and whorled leaves. The fruit consists of a pair of hard nutlets which separate when ripe. The coffee tree is related to them. The family also includes plants that yield valuable dyes.

Bedstraw, *Galium boreale,* is abundant nearly everywhere in the montane zone both on dry slopes and in meadows. It has numerous small white blossoms.

Three-flowered bedstraw, *Galium triflorum,* is much rarer. It has decumbent stems, few flowers, broader leaves, and grows in wet, shady places on rich soil. *Galium trifidum* has been found on the west side of the park.

HONEYSUCKLE FAMILY *(CAPRIFOLIACEAE)*

The plants of this family are mostly shrubs, all have opposite leaves; the fruit of each one found in the park except *Linnaea,* is a berry.

Twinflower, *Linnaea borealis* (fig. 148).—A dainty little trailing plant with opposite evergreen leaves and upright flower stems, each bearing a pair of pink, bell-shaped flowers. This plant is frequent in moist evergreen forests, where it often covers the ground with a mat of green foliage. It was named in honor of Linnaeus, the famous Swedish botanist.

Twinberry or **involucred honeysuckle,** *Lonicera involucrata.* — The park's only true, native honeysuckle. A shrub found on wet ground, especially in the subalpine zone, with large, ovate leaves 3 to 5 inches long, and pairs of yellow flowers, each pair surrounded by bracts that later enlarge, turn red, and enclose the two black, shiny berries.

Redberried elder, *Sambucus racemosa* ssp. *pubens* (fig. 149).—A low shrub of the montane and subalpine zones, with large clusters of small white flowers in June and early July, followed in late August by numerous small scarlet berries. The opposite leaves of this plant are pinnately compound, of several toothed and pointed leaflets.

Snowberry or **buckbrush,** *Symphoricarpos oreophilus.* — A low shrub along roadsides and on open slopes of the montane zone, with grayish, round or oblong leaves, and small pinkish flowers, followed by conspicuous white berries.

High bush cranberry, *Viburnum edule.*—A rather rare shrub in this region, found in moist thickets of the montane region. The opposite leaves are lobed and toothed, much resembling maple leaves; they also turn beautiful shades of red in autumn. The bush bears clusters of small white flowers in June, which are followed in August and September by red, acid berries. Often only two to three berries to a cluster mature.

ADOXA FAMILY *(ADOXACEAE)*

A family of small slender, smooth herbs with opposite thrice-compound leaves and small yellowish-green flowers in headlike clusters. *Adoxa moschatellina* has been found in a few places on moist ground. This is the only species in this family.

BELLFLOWER FAMILY *(CAMPANULACEAE)*

Plants with alternate leaves and attractive bell-shaped blue flowers.

Mountain harebell, *Campanula rotundifolia* (fig. 150). — A charming plant with several slender stems, each bearing a number of drooping blue bells. It is common throughout the mountainous region and is especially at home among rocks. It begins to bloom about the middle of summer and continues late into the autumn; occasionally a blossom is found in November. This is said to be the Scottish bluebell. In the tundra, dwarf plants with the normal size blossoms are found, as well as the **alpine harebell,** *Campanula uniflora,* a tiny plant with slenderer, darker blue flowers.

Parry harebell, *Campanula parryi* (fig. 151). — A slender, usually one-stemmed plant, with an erect violet or purple, funnel-shaped flower; the points of the five-lobed corolla are spreading. It is found in montane meadows.

Venus looking-glass, *Triodanis perfoliata,* is found at the eastern edge of the park. Its purple, saucer-shaped flowers occur in the axils of the clasping leaves.

VALERIAN FAMILY *(VALERIANACEAE)*

Tall plants with opposite leaves and small flowers. The characteristic thing about them is the arrangement of the corolla on top of the seed and the peculiar habit of the several long slender calyx lobes that are tightly inrolled at the time of flowering and do not become evident until the seeds begin to ripen. Then they start to uncurl and become conspicuous, for their inner side is covered with white hairs. When ripe, the seed is crowned with a ring of five to 15 spreading, feathery bristles. *Valeriana edulis* is a plant 18 inches to 5 feet tall, usually half its height consisting of the open, spreading inflorescence that has opposite branching. Found on moist slopes and in meadows of the montane zone. Its leaves are thick, seemingly parallel-veined and usually pinnately lobed. *Valeriana capitata,* a plant with a dense, umbellike cluster of white or pinkish flowers, is found in subalpine swamps. Its root has a very strong and disagreeable odor. *Valeriana occidentalis* is recorded from the western slope.

COMPOSITE FAMILY *(COMPOSITAE)*

This is the largest of all the families of flowering plants and contains about one-fifth of all seed plants growing in Rocky Mountain National Park. It is one of the groups in which the flower parts are most highly specialized and is also one of the most difficult families in which to distinguish the different individuals. For this reason, a short explanation of the structure of the flower-head is given here. This group includes many of the common weeds as well as many beautiful and showy wild flowers. While apparently very different, all of these plants have a similar arrangement of the flowers. What appears to be the "flower" of a sunflower is in reality an inflorescence made up of numerous small flowers closely packed together on the enlarged upper end of the stem, the *receptacle,* and surrounded by several or many *bracts.* These bracts form the *involucre* around the *head* of flowers. Superficially, they resemble a calyx made up of sepals (see fig. 2 of the Glossary).

Plants of this family have three different types of flower-heads. On this basis, the family is divided into three groups. The first group is made up of plants having two kinds of flowers. Around the margin of the head is a row of flowers with *ligulate,* that is, strapshaped, corollas. These are called *ray flowers,* and such flower-heads are said to be *radiate.* The center of the head, called the *disk,* is made up of flowers with short tubular, five-toothed corollas, called *disk flowers.* The ray flowers are often spoken of as "petals" when the flower-head is erroneously considered as one flower. The second group is composed of plants with flower-heads in which the flowers are all alike and are all disk flowers; all have tubular corollas. Such flower-heads are said to be *discoid.* The third group is made up of plants having flower-heads with flowers all alike but all ligulate, that is, all with long flat corollas.

Sunflowers and asters are examples of the first group, gayfeather *(Liatris)* of the second, and dandelions of the third. It is very easy to take a sunflower head apart and see the parts of each individual flower, but many members of this family have such tiny flowers that even the botanist cannot tell much about them without the use of a magnifying glass.

Composite plants have dry, one-seeded fruits which are technically called *achenes.* The calyx of the flower is a much modified structure called the *pappus.* It consists of a tuft of long soft hairs or of scales or bristles attached to the apex of the achene. Sometimes, it is hooked or barbed, or it may be small or entirely lacking. The pappus is often very conspicuous as the plant goes to seed. All these devices tend to insure wide distribution of the seeds as anyone who has watched dandelion or thistle seeds sail away on the wind can testify.

A. HEADS WITH BOTH RAY FLOWERS AND DISK FLOWERS

(AA, heads with only disk flowers, p. 124, AAA, heads with only ligulate flowers, p. 125)

B. Ray flowers white, blue, purple, or pinkish. (BB. Ray flowers yellow— (see below).)
    a. Plants stemless, blooming in early spring;
       leaves linear, grayish...................**Easter-daisy** (p. 125)
    aa. Plants with evident stems, but sometimes dwarf.
       b. Flower-heads aggregate in dense clusters, disks and rays white, plant aromatic; leaves very finely divided....**Yarrow** (p. 125)
       bb. Flower-heads not in dense clusters, disks yellow or reddish.
          c. Rays comparatively broad and few, involucral bracts of different lengths in several rows and overlapping (fig. 4 of Glossary).
            d. Involucral bracts with slender, recurved tips; rays reddish-purple...................**Tansy aster** (p. 126)
            dd. Involucral bracts flat; rays blue, violet or white, rarely reddish-purple.....................**Aster** (p. 125)
          cc. Rays comparatively narrow, very numerous, bracts in one or two rows of equal length
            (fig. 4 of Glossary)....................**Daisy** (p. 127)
BB. Ray flowers yellow.
    a. Disk flowers dark red and base of rays
       sometimes reddish.......................**Gaillardia** (p. 131)

Figure 147. **Alpine kittentail.**

Figure 148. **Twinflower.**

Figure 149. **Redberried elder.**

Figure 150. **Mountain harebell.**

Figure 151. **Parry harebell.**

Figure 152. **Easter-daisy, flower-heads about 1 inch broad, stemless.**

aa. Disk flowers yellow, brown, or nearly black.
    b. Leaves opposite.
        c. Pappus of slender bristles................**Arnica** (p. 131)
        cc. Pappus of awns or scales.............**Helianthus** (p. 138)
    bb. Leaves alternate.
        c. Disk flowers yellow or orange (cc. Disk flowers brown or blackish, p. 123).
            d. Lower leaves 8 to 12 inches long; heads 1 to 2 inches across, solitary or few.....**Golden curlyhead** (p. 136)
            dd. Lower leaves much shorter, or the heads many and small.
                e. Plant either rough-hairy or sticky in some part.
                    f. Leaves deeply divided; stems slightly sticky; rays nearly as wide as long...**Ragleaf bahia** (p. 131)
                    ff. Leaves not deeply divided, their margins entire, or wavy-toothed; rays much longer than wide.
                        g. Plant smooth below but buds very sticky; tips of involucral bracts bent out.......**Mountain gumweed** (p. 131)
                        gg. Plants rough-hairy throughout; tips of involucral bracts not bent out, sometimes slightly leafy................**Golden aster** (p. 131)
                ee. Plants neither very rough nor sticky, but sometimes woolly or hairy.
                    f. Plants of alpine situations; heads usually solitary on each flowering stem.
                      g. Plants densely white woolly at least at base; ligules three-toothed at apex.
                        h. Flowers 2 to 3 inches across; leaves divided.......**Rydbergia** (p. 133)
                        hh. Flowers smaller; leaves undivided.......**Woolly actinea** (p. 133)
                    gg. Plants not densely woolly; ligules entire at apex.
                      h. Plant woody at base.....**Tonestus** (p. 136)
                      hh. Plant soft and herbaceous at base......**Dandelion senecio** (p. 134)
                  ff. Plants not confined to alpine regions; heads usually several to many.
                    g. Bracts of the involucre in one series often black-tipped....**Ragworts** and **groundsels** (p. 133)
                    gg. Bracts of the involucre in two or more series, never black tipped.
                      h. Bracts loose and leafy; flower pale yellow.......**Parry goldenweed** (p. 136)
                      hh. Bracts tightly appressed, never leafy, flowers orange-yellow.**Goldenrod** (p. 136)
        cc. Disk flowers brown or blackish, at least darker than the rays.
            d. Disk elevated, cone-shaped, or cylindrical.
                e. Disk cylindrical, its height greater than its width.............**Coneflower** (p. 136)
                ee. Disk cone-shaped, its width greater than its height.
                    f. Plant rough-hairy, of medium size; leaves undivided; disk very dark brown.........**Black-eyed susan** (p. 136)

ff. Plant smooth, 3 to 6 feet high; leaves often lobed or divided; disk greenish or yellowish brown..........**Goldenglow** (p. 136)

dd. Disk flat or nearly so; at least some of the leaves opposite.

e. Plants perennial, native.

f. Plant bushy, many flowered; of sunny dry fields and hillsides.........**Dwarf sunflower** (p. 138)

ff. Plant slender, mostly unbranched; of meadows and aspen thickets...........**Helianthella** (p. 138)

ee. Plant annual, escaped from cultivation around ranches and along roads.......**Annual sunflower** (p. 138)

AA. HEADS WITH ONLY DISK FLOWERS
(AAA. Heads with only ligulate flowers, p. 125)

B. Foliage spine-tipped; corollas deeply cleft.

a. Heads purple...........................**Purple thistle** (p. 138)

aa. Heads cream-colored or dingy white.....**Colorado thistle** (p. 138)

BB. Foliage not spine-tipped.

a. Leaves opposite; plants 1 to 2 feet tall.....**Rayless arnica** (p. 131)

aa. Leaves alternate.

b. Heads erect, brightly colored or white.

c. Heads yellow.

d. Heads solitary, very compact; leaves three-parted...........**Gold buttons** (p. 131)

dd. Heads several to many.

e. Heads very small, numerous; a dwarf, fall-blooming shrub of open fields....**Dwarf rabbitbrush** (p. 138)

ee. Heads larger; plants never shrubs............**Turnip-leaved senecio** (p. 134)

cc. Heads not yellow.

d. Heads white, cream-colored, pink, or brownish; flowers "everlasting."

e. Plants blooming in spring, usually less than 10 inches high.........................**Catspaw** (p. 139)

ee. Plants blooming in summer and autumn, usually 1 foot or more high.

f. Heads pure white, papery...........**Pearly everlasting** (p. 139)

ff. Heads cream-colored, satiny ...**Cudweed** (p. 139)

dd. Heads bright purple, not "everlasting"; plant of open fields.......................**Gayfeather** (p. 139)

bb. Heads drooping.

c. Plant silvery with silky hairs; foliage finely cut, aromatic...........**Fringed mountain-sage** (p. 141)

cc. Plant not silvery.

d. Leaves triangular and toothed; heads yellowish; bracts pale green.........**Tasselflower brickellia** (p. 141)

dd. Leaves not triangular; disk yellow or greenish.

e. Bracts thick and purplish..**Bigelow groundsel** (p. 134)

ee. Bracts normal, green; leaves entire...........**Nodding senecio** (p. 134)

AAA. HEADS WITH ONLY LIGULATE FLOWERS, JUICE MILKY

B. Flower-heads pink or purplish, never yellow.
  a. Flowers pink, soon withering; heads solitary on the green, angled
    branches.............................**Milkpink** (p. 142)
  aa. Flowers purplish, in a long narrow raceme;
    stem unbranched..................**Rattlesnakeroot** (p. 142)
BB. Flower-heads yellow or white.
  a. Flower-heads yellow.
    b. Heads solitary, stems leafless.
      c. Involucre with black hairs.....**Alpine hawksbeard** (p. 141)
      cc. Involucre without black hairs.
        d. Leaves entire margined, broadest near the apex and
          tapering to the base....**Tall false-dandelion** (p. 141)
        dd. Leaves wavy-toothed, tapering
          to both ends............**Common dandelion** (p. 141)
    bb. Heads several.
      c. Pappus of soft, pure white hairs; involucres covered with
        light-colored, glandular hairs; plants of wet meadows and
        riverbanks......................**Hawksbeard** (p. 141)
      cc. Pappus of soft, dingy hairs; involucre covered with black
        hairs; plants of hillsides
        and fields.................**Slender hawkweed** (p. 141)
  aa. Flowers white or cream-colored; basal leaves with
    long white hairs...........**White-flowered hawkweed** (p. 141)

Easter-daisy, *Townsendia exscapa* (fig. 152). — Probably the earliest of all park flowers to bloom. It is found in late February on sunny sandy slopes in the foothills and may be expected in similar situations in April around Estes Park. The blossoms, which are an inch or more across, are clustered on the crowns of the plant nestled among the narrow grayish leaves. The rays are pale pink or white. *Townsendia grandiflora,* a plant with larger blossoms and stems 2 to 8 inches high, occurs sparingly on open fields, blooming in June and July.

Yarrow, *Achillea lanulosa.*—A plant of roadsides and fields with flat-topped clusters of small white flower-heads and leaves very finely dissected into numerous threadlike divisions. The foliage is very aromatic.

The common, white **ox-eye daisy,** *Chrysanthemum leucanthemum,* a widely distributed plant of European origin, is adventive along roads in the Grand Lake area.

Aster.—These plants are characterized by their imbricated involucre (fig. 4 of Glossary). The blue, purple, or white rays are comparatively few, often less than 30, and rather wide, usually ⅛-inch or more. The leaves are alternate and their margins entire except in the tansy aster.

Ray flowers white or whitish.
  Plants 2 to 5 feet tall; involucral bracts with prominent midribs; rays
    sometimes tinged pinkish or lavender;
    subalpine zone......................**Engelmann aster** (p. 126)

Plants less than 2 feet tall; involucral bracts without prominent midrib; montane zone.
  Foliage entirely smooth; stems tufted;
    freely branched . . . .**Porter aster** (p. 126)
  Foliage minutely but entirely pubescent; stems usually single from a running rootstock, but forming colonies;
    branches few, erect . . . .**Rough white aster** (p. 126)
Ray flowers blue, violet or purple.
  Ray flowers brilliant, reddish-purple or sometimes violet.
    Plant biennial, much branched, with
      many heads . . . . .Tansy aster (p. 126)
    Plant perennial, stems with few, erect branches, heads few.
      Heads usually solitary . . . . .Leafy bract aster (p. 126)
      Heads usually several . . . .**Western aster** (p. 127)
  Ray flowers usually blue, violet or pale lavender.
    Inflorescence a broad panicle, leaves
      narrow and sessile . . . .**Pacific aster** (p. 127)
    Inflorescence a constricted panicle.
      Leaves as broad, or nearly so at the base as at the middle; rays light blue; pappus white or cream-colored; stems
        often reddish . . . .**Sky-blue aster** (p. 127)
      Leaves much broader in the middle and tapering to both ends, the upper ones smaller . . . .**Smooth aster** (p. 127)

Engelmann aster, *Aster engelmannii.*—A coarse, stout plant 2 to 5 feet high, with leafy stems and clusters of white or lavender-tinged flowers, found on wet ground in the subalpine zone, especially between Bear and Nymph Lakes. The **glaucous aster,** *Aster glaucodes,* a smaller plant with oblong obtuse, spreading, glaucous leaves, also occurs.

Porter aster or **smooth white aster,** *Aster porteri.*—A branching plant 6 to 10 inches high, often growing in tufts, with smooth foliage and many flower-heads with white rays and yellow centers which turn dark red in age. It is abundant on open, sunny slopes and montane fields, blooming in August and September. Another white-rayed aster of less branching habit is the **rough white aster,** *Aster falcatus,* found on moister soil and coming into bloom 2 or 3 weeks later. Its foliage is roughened with small hairs. It grows from a running root stock. **Tansy aster,** *Aster bigelovii,* probably the most conspicuous purple aster, blooms profusely in late summer and autumn. It has many spreading branches and many flowers, with brilliant reddish-purple rays and yellow centers. The leaves are irregularly toothed. It grows abundantly in old fields, along roads, and around buildings, for it seems to thrive especially on disturbed soil. The plants are biennial, blooming the second year and then dying. The flowers begin to appear as early as the middle of July, and some plants are still blooming in October. The species is quite variable. *(Machaeranthera biglovii).*

Leafy-bract aster, *Aster foliaceus,* is a very variable plant. It may be from 1 to 3 feet tall. It has few comparatively large heads. The upper leaves are reduced in size and grade into the green loosely arranged involucral bracts. The rays are about ½-inch long and may be from rose to purple. The closely related

sun-loving aster, *Aster foliaceus* var. *apricus* (fig. 153), is a dwarf alpine plant with large, usually solitary, head and brilliant rose-purple or violet rays, often forming mats. It grows in exposed, stony situations of the alpine and subalpine regions.

Western aster, *Aster occidentalis,* a medium tall aster with several (not many), heads to each stem. Its rays are often the same beautiful reddish-purple as those of the sun-loving aster, but as is also the case with it, the rays may be blue or violet. The inner and outer involucral bracts of western aster are of about equal length.

Smooth aster, *Aster laevis,* with bright blue blossoms and smooth foliage, the lower leaves with winged petioles, the upper much smaller and with heart-shaped, clasping base, is found in meadows of the montane zone.

Pacific aster, *Aster chilensis (Aster adscendens),* with lavender or blue flowers, much branched inflorescence, and small narrow leaves, is found on fields and hillsides and along roads. *Aster campestris* has been collected at Shadow Mountain Reservoir.

Sky-blue aster, *Aster hesperius.* — A tall plant with beautiful sky-blue rays and long-oblong, pointed sessile leaves is common in meadows and along streams in the montane zone.

Daisy or **fleabane,** *Erigeron.* — A group of plants often mistaken for asters, from which they may be distinguished by the shape and arrangement of the involucral bracts and by the numerous long and extremely narrow rays. The showy plants of this genus are usually few-flowered and little-branched, and their stems are less rigid than those of the asters. The species may be distinguished by the following key:

A. Ray flowers conspicuous, fully as long as the width of the disk.
   B. Plant much-branched throughout, many-flowered;
           rays blue............................**Spreading daisy** (p. 128)
   BB. Plants mostly unbranched except in the inflorescence, flower-heads one
      to several on each stem.
        a. Involucre densely covered with pink or purplish-black hairs.
           b. Involucres covered with dark purplish or black hairs; rays
              usually white.................**Black-headed daisy** (p. 128)
          bb. Involucres densely pink woolly, rays
             pink or lavender ....**Beautiful daisy** (p. 128)
      aa. Involucres not woolly, or if densely hairy, hairs white.
        b. Plants 10 inches to 2 feet tall,[*] usually not caespitose.
          c. Leaves smooth.
            d. Rays wide, few, 50-70, tips of
              bracts loose...............**Subalpine daisy** (p. 128)
           dd. Rays narrow, tips of bracts usually appressed.
             e. Stems leafy, upper leaves smaller, ovate and sessile,
               rays 75-100, blue or violet.....**Aspen daisy** (p. 130)
             ee. Stems with few leaves, rays usually pale lavender,
               few, 40-80..................**Pale daisy** (p. 130)

[*]Heights given are intended to be average. There will always be some individual plants whose heights will be outside the figures given.

cc. Leaves pubescent, or at least their margins ciliate, rays
75-150.
e. Rays white, bracts with long, slender,
loose tips . . . .**Coulter daisy** (p. 130)
ee. Rays blue or purplish, involucres glandular.
f. Upper leaves glandular, tips of
bracts appressed . . . .**Greenes daisy** (p. 130)
ff. Upper leaves not, or only slightly, glandular, tips
of bracts loose . . . .**Dryland daisy** (p. 130)
bb. Plants usually less than 10 inches tall, often caespitose.
c. Leaves entire.
d. Plant spreading by runners, these not always evident
early in the season, heads pink in the bud, white when
open . . . .**Whiplash daisy** (p. 130)
dd. Plant without runners, flowerheads never pink in bud.
e. Plants of montane zone, foliage hairy.
f. Rays white . . . .**Dwarf daisy** (p. 130)
ff. Rays blue . . . .**Early blue daisy** (p. 130)
ee. Plants of alpine zone.
f. Involucre white-hairy . . . .**Arctic fleabane** (p. 130)
ff. Involucre and entire
plant smooth . . . .**Rockslide daisy** (p. 130)
cc. Leaves divided or definitely lobed.
d. Leaves three-parted, rays
usually white . . . .**Cut-leaved daisy** (p. 131)
dd. Leaves pinnately dissected,
rays usually violet . . . . . .**Pinnate-leaved daisy** (p. 131)
AA. Ray flowers inconspicuous, shorter than the width of the disk.
B. Plant widely branched: inflorescence in a
corymb or panicle . . . .**Bitter fleabane** (p. 131)
BB. Plant unbranched or with only a few, erect branches,
inflorescence a raceme . . . .**Spearleaf fleabane** (p. 131)

Spreading daisy, *Erigeron divergens.* — A densely hairy plant branched from the base, with many blue-rayed flower heads, blooming in August and September along roadsides and on open slopes below 9,000 feet.

Black-headed daisy, *Erigeron melanocephalus.* — A white-flowered daisy of the subalpine and alpine zones, easily recognized because of the black or purplish woolly hairs which cover the involucre; the stems are one-flowered, the leaves entire. It grows on snow accumulation areas and is frequently seen as an alpine plant with stems only a few inches high. Also sometimes found in subalpine meadows with stems nearly a foot high.

Beautiful daisy or **tall fleabane,** *Erigeron elatior* (fig. 155).—A lovely flower abundant in meadows of the subalpine zone, with large rose-colored heads; involucral bracts reddish and embedded in dense woolly hairs; rays numerous and very narrow; heads solitary or few. Blooms in August and is common at Bear Lake, Willow Park, Poudre Lakes, and elsewhere.

Subalpine daisy or **aster fleabane,** *Erigeron peregrinus.* — An exception in this genus because of its wide rays but easily recognized by the typical *Erigeron* involucre (fig. 4 of Glossary). It is one of the most conspicuous flowers of the subalpine meadows where its lavender or violet rays and orange-yellow disk are seen on every side in late July and August. It is usually one- to three-flowered. Occasionally the rays are white.

128

Figure 153. Sun-loving aster, stems about 4 - 8 inches tall.

Figure 154. Aspen daisy, plants 12 - 18 inches tall.

Figure 155. Beautiful daisy, 12 - 18 inches tall, pink wool on involucre.

Figure 156. Arctic fleabane, 3 - 6 inches tall.

Figure 157. Gaillardia, heads 2 - 4 inches broad.

Figure 158. Heartleaf arnica, heads about 3 inches broad.

Aspen daisy, *Erigeron speciosus* (fig. 154). — The commonest daisy of the montane zone; found in moist aspen groves and in meadows. It has smooth foliage and lavender to violet narrow rays and yellow disk. The stems are usually several-flowered. The variety *macranthus* is the commonest form in this region, but the typical form with narrower leaves also occurs.

Pale daisy, *Erigeron eximius.*—Commonly found in the subalpine zone with the beautiful and subalpine daisies, from which it may be distinguished by its paler color, its narrow rays, and lack of densely woolly involucre. It has nodding buds and clasping leaves.

Coulter daisy, *Erigeron coulteri,* with white rays and white hairy involucre, is one of the rarer plants of the park on the west side.

Greenes daisy, *Erigeron formosissimus,* a blue- or purplish-flowered daisy with leaves becoming smaller upwards, the uppermost are narrow with ciliate margins. Its stems are curved at the base.

Dryland daisy, *Erigeron subtrinervis,* is similar in appearance to the aspen daisy, but its stem and leaves are pubescent, its buds nod, and it grows in drier situations. *Erigeron glabellus* has also been found but seems quite rare.

Whiplash daisy or **trailing fleabane,** *Erigeron flagellaris.*—One of the commonest small daisies found below 10,000 feet. The rays are very narrow, almost threadlike, pink or red on the outside, so that the buds are always pink, but white when opened. The stems are slender and early in the season mostly leafless; the basal leaves are oblanceolate, acute, and entire. In June, it blooms profusely and then starts to produce runners with leaves evenly spaced along their whole length, and tufts of leaves at the tips, where the runner takes root and starts a new plant. It continues to bloom sparingly all summer and through September.

Dwarf daisy, *Erigeron pumilus.*—A white-flowered daisy with exceedingly hairy leaves and stems, growing from a stout woody root. The leaves are linear. It is occasionally found on dry slopes of the montane zone. The somewhat similar *Erigeron eatonii* occurs near Granby Reservoir.

Early blue daisy, *Erigeron vetensis.*—Similar to the whiplash and dwarf daisies but with blue ray flowers and foliage slightly less hairy and often somewhat sticky. The branches usually have one head. It is frequently seen on open slopes around Estes Park, blooming in June.

Arctic fleabane, *Erigeron simplex* (fig. 156).—An alpine daisy, with single heads and stems only a few inches high; rays violet and leaves entire; the involucre is covered with light-colored hairs. Found around most of the high lakes and on mountaintops.

Rockslide daisy, *Erigeron leiomeris,* is a low-growing plant of subalpine and alpine regions, usually found in loose rocks where its long, stout taproot anchors itself at considerable depth. This is usually divided into several branches at the crown so that the plant is loosely caespitose. Its foliage is entirely smooth. Each flowering-stem bears a single, blue-rayed head.

Cut-leaved daisy, *Erigeron compositus.*—Growing in tufts throughout the montane and sometimes higher, with white ray flowers and hairy leaves three-forked at the apex. It blooms throughout the summer but is most abundant in June. **Gold buttons,** *Erigeron compositus* var. *discoideus,* a variety without any ray flowers, is occasionally found growing with the species.

Pinnate-leaved daisy, *Erigeron pinnatisectus.*—A beautiful blue or violet daisy with pinnately divided leaves found in the alpine and upper subalpine regions. The stems are often only an inch or so high but the flower-heads are comparatively large, an inch or more across. Blooms in July and August.

In addition, the following **fleabane daisies** are found, but are less conspicuous because of their very short rays (they can be recognized by the characters given in the key on page 128): **bitter fleabane,** *Erigeron acris,* and **spearleaf fleabane,** *Erigeron lonchophyllus.*

Gaillardia, *Gaillardia aristata* (fig. 157). — This plant is one of the showy mountain flowers. The heads are 2 to 4 inches across with deep red or brownish disk and brilliant yellow rays. The rays are wide, tapering to the base, and three-toothed at apex. The leaves and stems are rough-hairy. It begins to bloom in July and is found throughout the summer from the foothills to timberline.

Arnica.—Rays and disk both yellow, leaves opposite. The latter character distinguishes these plants from most of the other yellow-flowered composites. Several species are found, all of which vary so much that determination is difficult.

Heartleaf arnica, *Arnica cordifolia* (fig. 158).—Large blossoms to 3 inches across and large basal, heart-shaped leaves; is very common in moist pine and spruce forests, blooming in May and June. The **daffodil arnica,** *Arnica latifolia,* with similar flowers but smaller and more numerous leaves, blooms abundantly in the subalpine zone in August and September. **Meadow arnica,** *Arnica fulgens,* a tall plant with narrow, strongly nerved leaves, is common in montane meadows. It has tufts of tawny hairs in the axils of the old leaves, at base of stems. **Rydberg arnica,** *Arnica rydbergii,* occurs in subalpine areas on the west side. Other species occurring in the park are **rayless arnica,** *Arnica parryi; Arnica mollis;* and **long-leaved arnica,** *Arnica longifolia.*

Ragleaf bahia, *Bahia dissecta* (fig. 159).—Plants 1 to 2 feet tall, branching, with golden yellow heads, the disk darker than the short, broad rays; leaves dissected into narrow segments; upper part of stem hairy and somewhat sticky.

Mountain gumweed, *Grindelia subalpina.*—A branching plant with numerous yellow flowers, easily recognized by the roundish buds that are covered on top with a white sticky substance. The involucral bracts have narrow curled tips. These plants look very untidy as they go to seed because of the numerous large sticky involucres and persistent withered rays.

Golden aster or **golden-eye,** *Chrysopsis villosa.*—Some forms of this species grow in the park, all rather similar. The flowers resemble asters but have yellow rays. The stems and leaves are covered with hairs which give the plants a grayish color and make them rough to the touch. There are usually several stems from the root crown, each one more or less branched. This is abundant from the foothills to timberline, especially on dry, sunny fields and hillsides. This plant is also called *Heterotheca villosa.*

Figure 159. **Ragleaf bahia, stems 1 - 2 feet tall.**

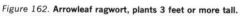

Figure 160. **Rydbergia, heads 2 - 4 inches broad, stems not over 6 inches tall.**

Figure 161. **Woolly actinea, plant alpine, cushion type.**

Figure 162. **Arrowleaf ragwort, plants 3 feet or more tall.**

Figure 163. **Wooton senecio.**

Rydbergia or **alpine sunflower,** *Hymenoxys grandiflora* (fig. 160).—One of the most striking plants of the rocky alpine ridges. Its lovely yellow flower-heads are 2 to 4 inches across on stems usually less than 6 inches high and sometimes only 1 to 2 inches high. The stems and the dissected leaves are covered with soft, loose white hairs. The yellow rays are three-toothed at apex. All the flower-heads always face in the same direction — east. This plant dies after blooming once.

Woolly actinea, *Hymenoxys acaulis* var. *caespitosa* (fig. 161).—A smaller plant than rydbergia with rather similar flower-heads, the yellow ligules are three-toothed, but leaves are entire; grows among rocks in exposed situations of the alpine tundra.

Ragwort, groundsel, or **senecio.**—A large group of plants similar in appearance and difficult to distinguish. A few have no ray flowers; the remainder have yellow or orange rays. The involucre is made up of one row of equal bracts with sometimes a few shorter bractlets at the base. The bracts are often black-tipped. The following key should help to distinguish those species most frequently encountered:

A. Flower-heads without rays.
    B. Heads ½-inch broad or more, drooping . . .**Bigelow groundsel** (p. 134)
    BB. Heads ⅓-inch broad or less.
        a. Heads somewhat drooping; leaves entire **Nodding senecio** (p. 134)
        aa. Heads erect; margins of
            leaves toothed. . . . .**Turnip-leaved senecio** (p. 134)
AA. Flower-heads with rays.
    B. Plants tall, 2 to 5 feet high; leaf margins finely but
        sharply toothed.
        a. Leaves long-triangular, broadest
            near the base. . . . .**Arrowleaf ragwort** (p. 134)
        aa. Leaves narrow, broadest in the middle, tapering
            to each end . . . .**Toothed ragwort** (p. 134)
    BB. Plants 2 feet or less in height.
        a. Foliage silvery white, plant mostly alpine . .**Hoary senecio** (p. 134)
        aa. Foliage green.
            b. Plant alpine, usually not over 6 inches high;
                heads solitary or few,
                usually drooping. . . . .**Dandelion senecio** (p. 134)
           bb. Plants subalpine or montane, usually over 6 inches tall;
                heads erect.
                c. Leaves with margins entire, or slightly wavy,
                    or with a few small teeth.
                    d. Plant with no woolly or cottony hairs.
                        e. Flower-heads few; plant of subalpine
                          meadows. . . . .**Thick-bracted senecio** (p. 135)
                      ee. Flower-heads many.
                          f. Leaves linear, occasionally with one or few
                            linear lobes . . . .**Broom senecio** (p. 135)
                          ff. Leaves obovate to oblanceolate,
                            never lobed . . . .**Wooton senecio** (p. 135)
                dd. Plant usually somewhat woolly; leaves not linear.
                    e. Heads very numerous; involucres about ⅛-inch
                      in diameter; bracts with conspicuous
                      black tips . . . .**Black-tipped senecio** (p. 135)

ee. Heads fewer; involucres about ¼-inch in
   diameter or more; peduncle of central head
   short . . . . **Lambstongue groundsel** (p. 135)
cc. Leaves, at least some of them, lobed or
   coarsely toothed.
   d. Leaves lobed half way to the midrib or deeper.
      e. Foliage and stem woolly; leaves with
         regular, comblike lobes,
         usually folded . . . . **Fendler senecio** (p. 135)
      ee. Foliage and stem not woolly, leaves flat.
         f. Leaves linear, sometimes with a few linear
            lobes . . . . **Broom senecio** (p. 135)
         ff. Leaves lanceolate in outline, pinnately
            dissected . . . . **Western golden ragwort** (p. 135)
   dd. Leaves irregularly toothed or shallowly lobed;
      plants of subalpine or alpine zones.
      e. Stems tufted, growing among rocks, rays
         yellow . . . . **Rock ragwort** (p. 135)
      ee. Stems usually single, growing in meadows;
         rays orange . . . . **Saffron ragwort** (p. 136)

Bigelow groundsel, *Senecio bigelovii.*—A plant of meadows and moist forests of the subalpine, rather rare, with a few large rayless, drooping heads; bracts purplish, disk yellow.

Nodding senecio, *Senecio pudicus.*—A plant with numerous small, light-yellow, or greenish heads, and dark-green leaves and stems. The lower leaves are broad, on long petioles, the upper leaves narrow and becoming sessile.

Turnip-leaved senecio, *Senecio rapifolius.*—Stems in groups, erect, each having a headlike, rounded cluster of small, erect, orange-yellow, discoid heads. The basal leaves are spatulate, or oblong, resembling turnip leaves, from which characteristic the plant takes its name. The middle and upper stem leaves are oblong, pointed, and sessile. All the leaves have sharply toothed margins.

Arrowleaf ragwort, *Senecio triangularis* (fig. 162).—A tall plant often 3 feet or more high, usually growing in clumps in wet ground of the subalpine region. The leaves are triangular and thickly toothed; the yellow, radiate heads are borne in corymblike clusters. This plant is often seen in August growing in dense clumps with the subalpine larkspur, the gold of the ragwort setting off the deep purple-blue of the larkspur. The **toothed ragwort,** *Senecio serra,* is similar, but its leaves are narrow and tapering.

Hoary senecio, *Senecio canus,* a beautiful silvery plant with golden yellow flower-heads, grows on stony or gravelly ground at high altitudes. Its leaves are entire, slightly toothed or sometimes lobed. *Senecio werneriaefolius* is a small plant, grayish when young, 2 to 6 inches tall with roundish or elliptic leaves that are usually toothed around the apex, and rather large heads that may be solitary or several together.

Dandelion senecio, *Senecio taraxacoides.*—A plant about 6 inches high, rather fleshy; leaves ovate or spatulate, more or less undulately lobed, margins toothed; midribs, petioles, and younger leaves purplish, sometimes woolly; heads one or few, large, an inch or more across; involucres purplish; rays light yellow, nearly ¼-inch wide. A taller species with long stalked, tilted heads, and spatulate toothed leaves is **daffodil senecio,** *Senecio amplectens* (fig. 164), found in subalpine meadows and at the edge of spruce forests. A similar but smaller tundra species, is **alpine senecio,** *Senecio holmii* (fig. 165), with light yellow rays at least twice as long as the involucre and toothed leaves which taper at both ends. *Senecio soldanella,* with rounded leaves and short ray flowers, is found in gravelly areas at very high altitudes. It has round or obovate leaves on long petioles and large solitary heads about 1 inch high.

Thick-bracted senecio, *Senecio crassulus.*—Two to five orange-yellow flower-heads; found in some subalpine meadows. Its basal leaves, when present, are spatulate or oblong with rounded apex; the remaining leaves acute at apex, the leaf margins mostly entire but occasionally showing a few very tiny teeth.

Wooton senecio, *Senecio wootonii* (fig. 163), a handsome plant with mostly basal leaves and neat, bright yellow flower-heads. The leaves are from 2 to 6 inches long, thick, more or less glaucous, and sometimes purplish, tapering at base into a winged petiole. In general, the rays are short and broad in comparison with other species of *Senecio*. This occurs in the Bear Lake region and on the west side.

Broom senecio, *Senecio spartioides.*—This rather bushy plant covered with numerous yellow-rayed flower-heads is common along roadsides, around buildings, and on fields of the montane region. Its leaves are very narrow, and some of them have a few narrow pinnate lobes projecting at right angles. It begins to bloom in late July and continues into September.

Black-tipped senecio, *Senecio atratus.*—Foliage and stem grayish with woolly hairs, leaves entire (or margins sometimes with very small teeth), flower-heads very numerous and small; involucral bracts with conspicuous black tips. Found on hillsides of the subalpine region, often along roadsides.

Lambstongue groundsel, *Senecio intergerrimus.*—A very variable plant. The most constant character is the very short peduncle of the central head. The plant is usually woolly with loose white hairs, the leaves entire or with a few small irregularities. It is an early blooming species, found on montane hillsides in May and June.

Fendler senecio, *Senecio fendleri.*—Somewhat similar to the lambstongue groundsel and often found with it, but the central peduncle not conspicuously shorter than the others, and the leaves pinnately lobed, the lobes resembling the teeth of a comb. In addition, the leaves are usually folded. This also begins to bloom in June in the montane and continues throughout the summer. It is frquently seen, occurring from the foothills to timberline.

Western golden ragwort, *Senecio eremophilus.*—This plant is conspicuous along the banks of the Bear Lake Road and on other roadsides and around dwellings. It is bushy and covered in mid-summer with bright yellow flower-heads. When it goes to seed, it is still conspicuous because of the white pappus of the achenes. The leaves are dark green, smooth, and deeply pinnately lobed. The **rock ragwort,** *Senecio carthamoides,* a rather similar plant found in subalpine and alpine rockslides, has tufts of leafy stems, each bearing one or more large flower-heads with light yellow rays.

Saffron ragwort, *Senecio crocatus.*—One of the commonest plants in many wet subalpine meadows and alpine snow accumulation areas, where its orange rays make it conspicuous. The upper leaves clasp the stem by a broad base and are abruptly narrowed near the middle, with a tapering point. All the leaves are more or less lobed or toothed. A similar plant with yellow rays is *Senecio dimorphophyllus.*

Goldenweed, *Haplopappus.*—The plants in this genus differ strongly from each other in general appearance. Their similarities are that they all have yellow or orange ray and disk flowers, and those in the park all have green, loosely overlapping involucral bracts.

Parry goldenweed, *Haplopappus parryi,* is a plant of lodgepole forests, meadows and aspen groves with light green foliage and pale yellow rays; stems from a slender, running rootstock. It blooms in August.

Alpine goldenweed or **tonestus,** *Haplopappus pygmaeus.*—This plant is only a few inches high with a compact, leafy, woody stem. Its bright yellow rays are entire, and its dark green foliage is smooth. *Haplopappus lyallii* is similar but differs in being very glandular. Both grow in exposed situations, usually among rocks in the alpine tundra. **Golden curlyhead,** *Haplopappus crocea,* a plant 10 to 24 inches tall with orange rays that tend to curl backward as the flowers age, is found in montane and subalpine meadows of the western slope.

Goldenrod.—The goldenrod species are difficult to distinguish in the field but easily recognized as a group. The common one seen among rocks and along trails at higher altitudes with the flower spray rounded, is **dwarf goldenrod,** *Solidago spathulata.* The reduced alpine form of this is var. *nana.* The common species of roadsides with flower sprays somewhat one-sided and recurved is *Solidago nemoralis (Solidago sparsiflora).* The tall one of streambanks and wet meadows of the lower valleys is **giant goldenrod,** *Solidago gigantea.* In addition, the following species occur in the park: *Solidago multiradiata,* in which the bases of the leaves are fringed with hairs, and **smooth goldenrod,** *Solidago missouriensis,* and *Solidago canadensis* in the Never Summer Range.

Black-eyed susan, *Rudbeckia hirta* (fig. 166), well known for its large gold and chocolate flower-heads and rough foliage, is frequently seen in mountain meadows. It may be distinguished from gaillardia, which it is sometimes considered to resemble, by the shape of the rays that taper to the apex and the lack of the three distinct teeth of gaillardia as well as the smooth cone-shaped disk.

Goldenglow or **cutleaf coneflower,** *Rudbeckia laciniata* (fig. 167). — A very tall, smooth plant with large flower-heads 2 to 4 inches across, drooping yellow rays, and a raised, greenish-yellow disk. It is frequent along streams of the montane zone. *Rudbeckia montana,* a rayless species, is recorded from Grand Lake.

Prairie coneflower, *Ratibida columnaris,* with yellow or purplish rays and a dark cylindric or columnar receptacle up to 1½ inches tall, is a foothill plant sometimes seen along the eastern edge of the park.

Figure 164. **Daffodil senecio.**

Figure 165. **Alpine senecio.**

Figure 167. **Goldenglow, plants 4 - 6 feet tall, rays drooping.**

Figure 166. **Black-eyed susan.**

Figure 168. **Aspen sunflower, heads 3 - 4 inches broad.**

Figure 169. **Salsify, flower.**

Figure 170. **Salsify, fruiting head.**

Dwarf sunflower, *Helianthus pumilus.*—A perennial bushy plant, very rough-hairy, bearing numerous "sunflowers" 1 to 2 inches across, with bright yellow rays and dull yellow or brownish disks. It is abundant on open rocky slopes below 9,000 feet. The **annual sunflower,** *Helianthus annuus,* adventive in the park, a taller plant with larger heads, is seen along roadsides and around ranches.

Aspen sunflower or **five-nerve helianthella,** *Helianthella quinquenervis* (fig. 168).—A tall, slender plant with one or few large flower-heads 3 to 4 inches across, pale-yellow rays, and brownish or greenish-yellow disk. The long, tapering leaves are mostly five-nerved. This plant is most frequently seen on damp soil in aspen groves of the montane zone, though it is occasionally found in meadows or in open spruce forests. **Parrys aspen sunflower,** *Helianthella parryi,* is found on the western slope. **Balsamroot,** *Balsamorhiza sagittata,* grows abundantly at lower elevations of the western slope.

Thistle, *Cirsium.*—Nearly everyone is familiar with these plants, which are easily recognized by the lobed, spiny leaves and by the typical thistle flower-heads. These heads are discoid, but the tubular corollas are exceptionally long and split into narrow divisions so that the head has a looser appearance than most discoid flower-heads.

Purple thistle, *Cirsium undulatum.*—Frequently seen around buildings, along roadsides, and on open fields. Its foliage is whitened with woolly hairs, which disappear as the leaves get older, and the heads are a beautiful rose-purple.

Colorado thistle, *Cirsium coloradense.*—The several heads are whitish or cream-colored; found in meadows and along streambanks. Its variety, *Cirsium coloradense* var. *acaulescens,* the stemless thistle, with the flower-heads sessile in a basal rosette of leaves, is found in rockslides of the subalpine and alpine zones and occasionally in lower meadows.

Others found in the park are: **American thistle,** *Cirsium centaureae,* with medium-sized, whitish heads, the involucral bracts somewhat fringed along their edges; **Rocky Mountain thistle,** *Cirsium scopulorum,* with sessile heads, flowers pinkish or pale purple and woolly bracts with spines on their edges as well as one at the tip of each. The last is a high altitude plant and has much the same habit as the Colorado thistle, the stems sometimes being very short. They may be distinguished because the bracts of the latter lack the woolliness and lateral spines of the former. *Cirsium engelmannii,* with long-peduncled, rose-purple heads, and *Cirsium bipinnatum,* also with purple heads, have been reported.

Canada thistle, *Cirsium arvense,* a very troublesome weed that spreads from underground rootstocks has recently appeared along roadsides and in moist meadows of the park. Its numerous, small, purple flower-heads make masses of it rather attractive in appearance when in bloom. **Tweedy thistle,** *Cirsium tweedyi,* is reported in the park.

Dwarf rabbitbrush, *Chrysothamnus viscidiflorus.*—This bushy plant, usually not over a foot high, becomes conspicuous in late August and September on open fields of the montane zone. Its leaves are linear and often somewhat twisted; its numerous tiny yellow heads are held erect. *Chrysothamnus parryi* is found at the edge of the park on the western side.

Catspaw or **pussytoes,** *Antennaria.*—Plants related to the everlasting flowers, with white or silvery foliage and oblong or oval flower-heads, the inner bracts of which are papery, either white, pink, or brownish. They usually grow in mats and spread by leafy stolons.

Rocky Mountain pussytoes, *Antennaria parvifolia.*—One of the most abundant plants of the open fields. It forms large mats of whitish foliage and in May sends up short stems 2 to 4 inches high, bearing several heads with white or rarely pinkish, papery bracts. The leaves are rounded, tapering to a broad petiole, or spatulate-shaped. The **alpine catspaw,** *Antennaria alpina,* similar to the Rocky Mountain pussytoes but with brownish bracts, has also been found.

Showy pussytoes, *Antennaria anaphaloides.*—A plant 6 to 10 inches tall having long whitish leaves with distinct parallel nerves; sometimes found on partly shaded hillsides, blooming in July and August.

Pussytoes, *Antennaria rosea.* — Stems 4 to 8 inches tall; heads oval, inner bracts bright rose, pink, or white. In the park, this plant seems to be common in the montane and subalpine zones, and *Antennaria corymbosa* occasionally occurs in wet subalpine meadows.

Pearly everlasting, *Anaphalis margaritacea.*—Very abundant on the burned-over lands of the subalpine zone, especially around Bear Lake and along the upper part of the Fall River Road. The stems are usually about a foot high, the leaves narrowly lanceolate or linear, green above; the stems and underside of leaves are white with soft, loose cottony hairs; heads numerous, corymbosely clustered; bracts pure white, papery.

Cudweed, *Gnaphalium chilense (G. decurrens).*—Less abundant than the pearly everlasting, but rather similar in general appearance. The stem is yellowish-green and sticky, at least on the lower part, rather than white-cottony, and the bracts are cream-colored and satiny. *Gnaphalium grayi,* a smaller, inconspicuous plant, grows on wet ground.

Gayfeather or **blazing star,** *Liatris punctata.* — This plant grows in tufts on the open fields where its spikes of brilliant purple, feathery flower-heads make it conspicuous. Another species with fewer but larger heads is *Liatris ligulistylis.*

Mountain-sage or **wormwood,** *Artemisia.* — A very large genus with many representatives in this region. Most of them are inconspicuous, as their flower-heads are very small and never brightly colored. They are in no way related to the true sage *(Salvia)* of which there are no representatives in the park. Most of the wormwoods have a very bitter sap, and many of them a pleasantly aromatic odor. The involucral bracts are often edged with dark brown or black. Many of these plants have very attractive silvery foliage.

Sagebrush or **big sagebrush,** *Artemisia tridentata* (fig. 2).—In a dwarf condition, this plant is found in colonies in a few places in the park on the eastern side of the Continental Divide, especially in Glacier Basin, on the south and west slopes of Deer Mountain, and around Horseshoe Park. It is a woody shrub, rarely over a foot high in this vicinity, with wedge-shaped, three-toothed, silvery leaves. On the western slope around Grand Lake it is more abundant and grows to a greater size, and another species with longer, entire leaves, *Artemisia cana,* is found with it.

Figure 171. Montane meadow, Rocky Mountain iris and meadow arnica, ponderosa pine in background.

Figure 172. View of subalpine lake, meadows, flowers, paintbrush, daisies and others.

Figure 173. Alpine flower garden with Mummy Mountain.

Figure 174. Alpine flower garden.

Fringed mountain-sage, *Artemisia frigida.*—Tufts of silvery, fringed leaves and slender racemes of nodding yellow flower-heads; abundant throughout the park, especially among rocks. The aromatic heads of this plant were used by the early mountaineers to make a very bitter tea that was considered an excellent tonic and a remedy for mountain fever. A somewhat similar species with less finely cut leaves, *Artemisia coloradensis,* is often found intermingled with it.

Rock mountain-sage, *Artemisia scopulorum,* is one of the commonest plants in the tundra. **Patterson mountain-sage,** *Artemisia pattersonii,* is very much like it but is usually smaller and has a larger terminal head and only two or three smaller heads. **Arctic mountain-sage,** *Artemisia arctica* ssp. *saxicola,* grows in snow accumulation areas of the tundra. **Alpine mountain-sage,** *Artemisia borealis,* distinguished by its rosy red stem, is also found in the tundra.

The following additional species grow in the park: *Artemisia ludoviciana* and var. *gnaphalodes; Artemisia dracunculus; Artemisia canadensis;* and *Artemisia biennis.*

Alpine hawksbeard, *Crepis alpicola.*—A plant of the alpine zone usually with only one flower-head and no leaves on the stem. The yellow flowers are all ligulate, the involucre covered with black hairs. Another species of hawksbeard found in the park, usually in montane meadows, is *Crepis runcinata.*

Burnt-orange dandelion, *Agoseris aurantiaca.*—The flowers are dark orange, the leaves dark green and entire. The plant is found on moist soil of the subalpine region.

Tall false-dandelion, *Agoseris glauca.* — Large yellow heads resembling the common dandelion but with leaves pale green and usually not much lobed; found around ranches and roadsides below 9,000 feet. This is a variable species. Some individuals may have distinctly toothed leaves, some may be more or less hairy, some may have the involucral bracts spotted with black.

Rock dandelion, *Taraxacum lyratum.*—A diminutive plant, stem usually less than 2 inches high, with leaves resembling the common dandelion, and small yellow heads, is sometimes found among rocks in the alpine region. Found also in the alpine are *Taraxacum phymatocarpum* and *Taraxacum ceratophorum,* which are somewhat larger.

Common dandelion, *Taraxacum officinale,* has been introduced in this region where it thrives well and is very abundant around dwellings and in meadows.

Slender hawkweed, *Hieracium gracile.*—A plant with a basal rosette of obovate or spatulate leaves from which rises a slender stem bearing one to three pale yellow flower-heads with black-hairy involucres. **White-flowered hawkweed,** *Hieracium albiflorum,* is similar but does not have any black hairs. Its flowers are whitish, and the basal leaves have long white hairs.

Tasselflower brickellia, *Brickellia grandiflora,* with drooping, cream-colored rayless heads, occurs on rocky foothill slopes.

Salsify, *Tragopogon dubius* (figs. 169 and 170), a tall, coarse plant with dandelion-like flower-heads and beautiful, round seed clusters, is common on open areas at lower altitudes.

Sweet coltsfoot, *Petasites sagittata,* a rare plant of cold bogs, with large arrowhead-shaped leaves, dark green on their upper surfaces but white beneath, has been found near Grand Lake.

Rattlesnakeroot, *Prenanthes racemosa.*—An interesting plant found occasionally in open, moist woods and meadows. It has an erect stem with several pendant rose or purplish heads.

Milkpink or **skeleton weed,** *Lygodesmia juncea.*—A branched plant with bare, green stems and flat, pink flower-heads sometimes found at lowest elevation in the park.

Carelessweed or **horseweed,** *Iva xanthifolia,* is a tall coarse plant with clusters of small green flowers and leaves like sunflower leaves, sometimes seen around settlements.

Spiny sow-thistle, *Sonchus asper,* with yellow flowers like small dandelions and prickle-edged leaves, is an introduced weed seen on waste ground.

Slender thelesperma, *Thelesperma megapotamicum (Thelesperma gracile),* with dark, rayless flower-heads and inner involucral bracts fused into a cup, has been found on open montane fields.

Glossary

Figures 1 through 3 of this Glossary have been reproduced in this publication
with the permission of the Museum of Northern Arizona, Flagstaff, Ariz.

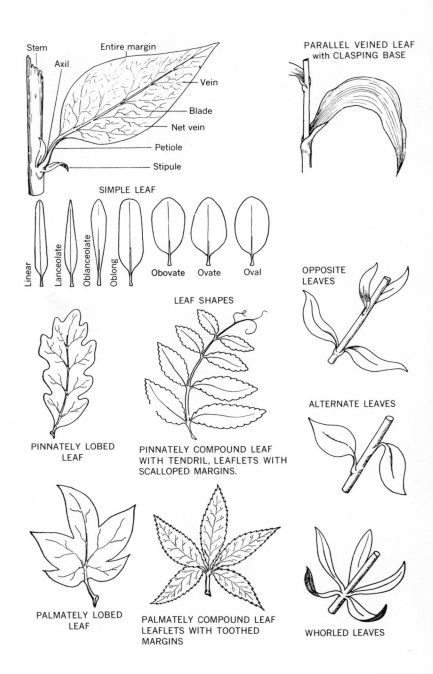

Stem

Entire margin

Axil

Vein

Blade

Net vein

Petiole

Stipule

PARALLEL VEINED LEAF
with CLASPING BASE

SIMPLE LEAF

Linear

Lanceolate

Oblanceolate

Oblong

Obovate

Ovate

Oval

LEAF SHAPES

OPPOSITE
LEAVES

PINNATELY LOBED
LEAF

PINNATELY COMPOUND LEAF
WITH TENDRIL, LEAFLETS WITH
SCALLOPED MARGINS.

ALTERNATE LEAVES

PALMATELY LOBED
LEAF

PALMATELY COMPOUND LEAF
LEAFLETS WITH TOOTHED
MARGINS

WHORLED LEAVES

Figure 1

144

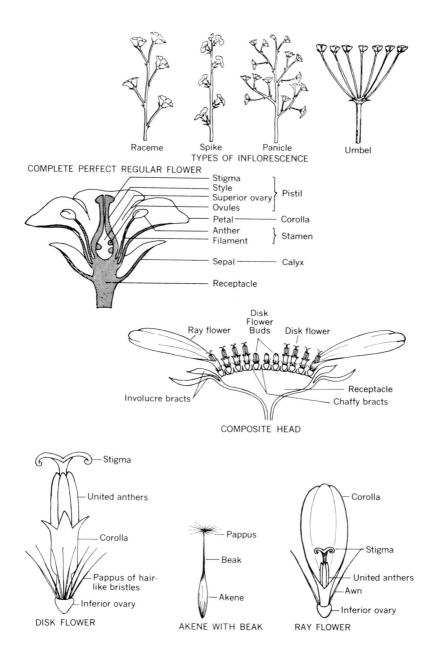

Raceme   Spike   Panicle   Umbel

TYPES OF INFLORESCENCE

COMPLETE PERFECT REGULAR FLOWER

Stigma
Style
Superior ovary } Pistil
Ovules
Petal ——————— Corolla
Anther
Filament } Stamen
Sepal ——————— Calyx
Receptacle

Disk
Flower
Buds
Ray flower   Disk flower

Receptacle
Involucre bracts   Chaffy bracts

COMPOSITE HEAD

— Stigma

— United anthers

— Corolla

— Pappus of hair-
  like bristles
— Inferior ovary

DISK FLOWER

— Pappus

— Beak

— Akene

AKENE WITH BEAK

— Corolla

— Stigma

— United anthers
— Awn
— Inferior ovary

RAY FLOWER

Figure 2

145

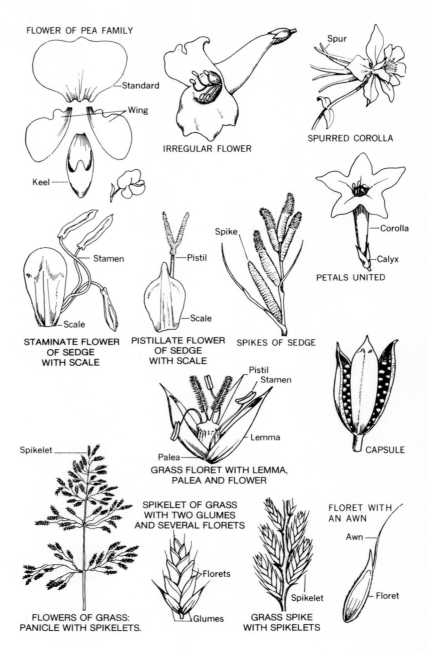

FLOWER OF PEA FAMILY

Standard

Wing

Keel

IRREGULAR FLOWER

Spur

SPURRED COROLLA

Stamen

Scale

STAMINATE FLOWER
OF SEDGE
WITH SCALE

Pistil

Scale

PISTILLATE FLOWER
OF SEDGE
WITH SCALE

Spike

SPIKES OF SEDGE

Corolla

Calyx

PETALS UNITED

Pistil
Stamen

Lemma

Palea

GRASS FLORET WITH LEMMA,
PALEA AND FLOWER

CAPSULE

Spikelet

FLOWERS OF GRASS:
PANICLE WITH SPIKELETS.

SPIKELET OF GRASS
WITH TWO GLUMES
AND SEVERAL FLORETS

Florets

Glumes

Spikelet

GRASS SPIKE
WITH SPIKELETS

FLORET WITH
AN AWN

Awn

Floret

Figure 3

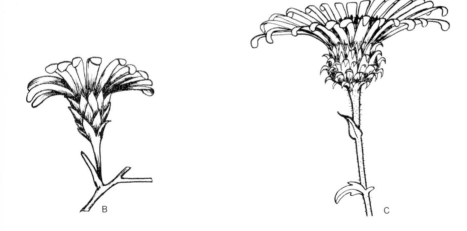

Comparison of involucres of some composites. (A) Daisy *(Erigeron)*,
(B) Aster *(Aster)*,
(C) Tansy aster *(Aster bigelovii)*.

Drawings by L. W. Durrell.

Figure 4

Definitions

Achene. A small, dry, hard, one-celled, one-seeded, nonsplitting fruit.

Acuminate. Taper-pointed.

Acute. Sharp-pointed or ending in a point less than a right angle.

Adnate. United in growth; the calyx is adnate to the seedpod in the bluebell family.

Adventive. Plants of foreign origin becoming naturalized in this region.

Alpine zone. That region above timberline, usually above 11,500 feet. See fig. 7.

Alternate. (Used of leaves, branches, etc.) Occurring singly at the nodes.

Ament. See catkin.

Annual. Of only 1 year's duration.

Anther. The essential part of the stamen that contains the pollen.

Aquatic. Growing in water.

Awl-shaped. Sharp-pointed from a broader base.

Axil. The upper angle between a leaf and the stem.

Axillary. Occurring in the axils.

Axis. The central line of any body; the organ around which others are attached.

Bract. In general the leaves of an inflorescence, more or less different from ordinary leaves; always sessile; especially the small leaf or scale in the axil of which a flower or its pedicel stands.

Bulblet. A small bulb, especially one borne upon the stem or in the inflorescence.

Caespitose. Growing in turflike patches or tufts.

Calyx. The outer circle of floral leaves, made up of the *sepals* which may be either distinct or joined together. If only one circle is present, it is called a calyx even though it is showy and appears like a corolla. See fig. 2 of Glossary.

Carpel. The unit of structure of the pistil, which may consist of a single carpel or of several carpels.

Catkin. A scaly spike of small flowers of which the pussy willow is a typical example. Also called an ament.

Ciliate. Beset on the margin with a fringe of hairs.

Corolla. The inner circle of floral leaves, usually showy. It is made up of *petals,* which may be either united or separate. It is always surrounded by a calyx. See fig. 2 of Glossary.

Corymb. A flat or convex flower cluster, with branches arising at different levels and flowers blooming at the outer edges first.

Cotyledons. The seed leaves, the first leaves of the embryo.

Crenate. (Of margins of leaves and petals.) With rounded teeth; scalloped. See fig. 1 of Glossary.

Deciduous. Falling off or subject to fall; applied to plants whose leaves fall in autumn.

Decumbent. Reclined on the ground, the summit tending to rise.

Dentate. Toothed.

Dicotyledonous. Used of plants which have a pair of cotyledons in the embryo.

Dioecious. Unisexual, with the two kinds of flowers on separate plants.

Disk. The face of any flat body; the central region of a head of flowers, like the sunflower, as opposed to the *ray* or margin; a fleshy expansion of the receptacle of a flower.

Dissected. Cut deeply into many lobes or divisions.

Ecology. The study of plants in relation to other living things and their environment.

Entire. The margin not at all toothed, notched or divided. See fig. 1 of Glossary.

Evergreen. Holding the leaves over winter or longer, until new ones appear.

Exserted. Protruding out of, as the stamens out of the corolla.

Fertile. Fruit bearing, or capable of producing fruit; also applied to anthers when they produce good pollen.

Filament. The stalk of a stamen; also any slender thread-shaped appendage. See fig. 2 of Glossary.

Floret. A small flower, usually one of a dense cluster. See fig. 3 of Glossary.

Frond. The leaf of ferns.

Genus, plural *Genera.* A group of plants made up of closely related species.

Glabrous. Smooth, having no hairs, bristles, or other pubescence.

Glaucous. Covered with a fine white powder that rubs off (bloom), like that on a fresh plum or a cabbage leaf. It often gives foliage a bluish appearance.

Glume. The outer sterile bract of a grass spikelet. One or two form the base of each spikelet. See fig. 3.

Habitat. The situation in which a plant grows.

Herb. A plant with no persistent woody stem above ground.

Herbaceous. With the texture of common herbage; not woody. Applied to plants which are herbs as distinguished from those which are shrubs or trees.

Imbricated. Overlapping (as shingles on a roof), either vertically or spirally, where the lower piece covers the base of the next higher; or laterally as in the arrangement of a calyx or corolla, where at least one piece must be wholly external and one internal.

Imperfect flowers. Lacking either stamens or pistils.

Indusium. The shield or covering of the sorus ("fruit-dot") of a fern.

Inferior. Applied to the seedpod when the calyx and corolla are placed on top of it instead of being inserted at its base inclosing it.

Inflorescence. The flowering part of a plant and especially the mode of its arrangement. See fig. 2 of Glossary.

Involucre. A whorl or set of bracts around a flower, umbel, or head. See fig. 4 of Glossary.

Irregular. Used to describe a calyx or corolla in which all the parts are not alike. Violets and sweetpeas are examples of irregular flowers, while a wild rose is a regular flower. See fig. 3 of Glossary.

Keel. Used to describe the two lower petals of flowers of the pea family; also any projecting ridge on a surface, like the keel of a boat. See fig. 3 of Glossary.

Lanceolate. Lance-shaped. See fig. 1 of Glossary.

Leaflet. One of the divisions or blades of a compound leaf.

Lemma. The outer and usually larger bract of the grass flower. See fig. 3 of Glossary.

Linear. Narrow and flat, the margins parallel. See fig. 1 of Glossary.

Lobe. Any projection or division (especially a rounded one) of a leaf, etc.; used also of the divisions of a united corolla.

-merous. Referring to the number of parts of the flower.

Midrib. The middle or main rib of a leaf. See fig 1 of Glossary.

Monocotyledonous. Used of plants that have only one cotyledon in the embryro.

Montane zone. The region between 6,000 and 9,000 feet, which contains mostly a mixed forest of western yellow pine and Douglas-fir, with lodgepole pine or aspen coming in on burned areas above 8,000 feet, also aspen groves and many open fields and hillsides. See figs. 1 and 2.

Naturalized. Introduced from a foreign country, but growing wild and propagating freely by seed.

Needle-shaped. Long, slender and rigid, like the leaves of pines.

Node. A knot; the joints of a stem, from which the leaves arise.

Obovate. The broad end upward, inversely ovate. See fig. 1 of Glossary.

Opposite. Applied to leaves and branches when an opposing pair occurs at each node. See fig. 1 of Glossary.

Ovary. That part of the pistil which contains the ovules (young seeds). See fig. 2 of Glossary.

Ovate. Shaped like the section of an egg, with the broader end downward. See fig. 1 of Glossary.

Palea. The inner and usually smaller bract of the grass flower. See fig. 3 of Glossary.

Palmate. Applied to a leaf whose leaflets, divisions, or main ribs all spread from the apex of the petiole, like a hand with outspread fingers. See fig. 1 of Glossary.

Panicle. An open or dense cluster in which the secondary branches are branched again. Is usually used of an inflorescence. See fig. 2 of Glossary.

Papilionaceous. Butterfly-shaped; applies to such a corolla as that of the pea or bean. See fig. 3 of Glossary.

Pedicel. The stalk of each particular flower of a cluster.

Peduncle. A flowerstalk, whether of a single flower or of a flower cluster.

Pendent. Hanging.

Perennial. Lasting from year to year.

Perfect. A flower containing both pistil and stamens. The calyx and corolla are not necessarily present.

Perianth. The floral envelopes of the flower; especially when the sepals and petals cannot be distinguished, as in many plants of the lily family.

Petal. A constituent member of the corolla. (See *corolla.*)

Petaloid. Petallike; resembling or colored like petals.

Petiole. The leaf-stalk.

Pinna, plural *pinnae.* One of the divisions of a pinnately divided leaf, used especially of ferns.

Pinnate. Leaflets disposed along the main axis of the leaf; feather-veined (secondary veins arising from a midrib). See fig. 1 of Glossary.

Pinnately lobed, cleft, parted, divided, etc. The varying depths of division of a pinnate (feather-veined) leaf. See fig. 2 of Glossary.

Pistil. The seed-bearing organ of the flower. It is made up of the *ovary,* which becomes the seedpod, the *style,* and the *stigma.* See fig. 2 of Glossary.

Plumose. Plumed or feathery.

Pollen. Pollen grains; the male element in flowering plants which must be deposited on the stigma of the pistil in order that the ovules may be fertilized and develop into seeds.

Polygamous. With both perfect and imperfect flowers on the same plant.

Produced. Extended or projecting, as the upper sepal of a larkspur is *produced* above into a spur.

Pubescence. Fine and soft hairs.

Pubescent. Covered with fine, soft hairs.

Raceme. A flower cluster with one-flowered pedicels along the axis of inflorescence. See fig. 2 of Glossary.

Rachis. An axis bearing close-set organs; especially the midrib of a fern frond.

Radiate. Furnished with ray flowers.

Ray. The marginal flower of a head or cluster when different from the rest, especially when ligulate; the branch of an umbel.

Receptacle. The more or less expanded or produced end of an axis which bears the organs of a flower or the collected flowers of a head. See fig. 2 of Glossary.

Reflexed. Bent outward or backward.

Regular. Used to describe a calyx or corolla in which all the parts are similar; radially symmetrical.

Rudimentary. Imperfectly developed, or in an early stage of development.

Runner. A slender and prostrate branch rooting at the end or at the joints. Strawberries are examples of plants having such *runners.*

Sepal. A constituent member of the calyx. See fig. 2 of Glossary.

Serrate. Serrated. With margin cut into teeth pointing forward. See fig. 1 of Glossary.

Sessile. Without any stalk, as a leaf destitute of petiole, a flower destitute of pedicel, or an anther destitute of filament.

Shrub. A woody perennial, smaller than a tree, usually with several stems.

Silky. Glossy with a coat of soft fine, close-appressed, straight hairs.

Silvery. Shining white or bluish gray, usually from a silky pubescence.

Simple. Of one piece, opposed to compound.

Sorus, plural *sori.* The "fruit-dots" of ferns, a cluster of little sacs, each of which contains many spores. Sori usually occur in characteristic arrangement on the back of the fertile frond.

Spatulate. Gradually narrowed downward from a rounded summit.

Species. A group containing all the individuals of a particular kind of plant.

Spicate. Arranged in or resembling a spike.

Spike. A form of simple inflorescence with the flowers sessile or nearly so upon a more or less elongated common axis. See fig. 3 of Glossary.

Spikelet. Part of an inflorescence, especially in grasses. See fig. 3 of Glossary.

Stamen. The pollen-bearing organ, made up of the *filament* and the *anther* that contains the pollen. See fig. 2 of Glossary.

Stigma. The region of the pistil that receives the pollen.

Stipules. The appendages on each side of the base of certain leaves.

Style. The beaklike prolongation of the pistil above the ovary, which bears the stigma. See fig. 2 of Glossary.

Subalpine zone. The region between 9,500 feet and timberline containing heavy Engelmann spruce-alpine fir forest, meadows, and bogs. On the exposed ridges will be found a stunted growth of limber pine, and on the burned areas lodgepole pine or aspen. In general, this zone supports the most luxuriant plant life of the mountains. (See fig. 14.)

Superior. Used of the ovary when the other parts of the flower are inserted at its base or below it, as in the buttercup family.

Ternate. Arranged in threes.

Timberline. The region on mountains where tree growth stops due to severe climatic conditions, and above which only herbs and dwarf shrubs are found. The last trees are often much deformed by the high winds and quite frequently become prostrate. The term "tree limit" is sometimes used. See fig. 5.

Umbel. The umbrellalike form of inflorescence in which the peduncles or pedicels all arise from one point. See fig. 2 of Glossary.

Whorl. A group of three or more similar organs radiating from a node. See fig. 1 of Glossary.

SELECTED REFERENCES

BAILEY, VIRGINIA LONG, and HAROLD EDWARDS BAILEY. 1949. *Woody Plants of the Western National Parks*. American Midland Naturalist, Monograph No. 4.

CHASE, AGNES. 1959. *First Book of Grasses*. Smithsonian Institution, Washington, D. C.

COULTER, JOHN M., and AVEN NELSON. 1909. *New Manual of Botany of the Central Rocky Mountains*. American Book Co., New York.

CRAIGHEAD, JOHN J., FRANK C. CRAIGHEAD, and RAY J. DAVIS. 1963. *A Field Guide to Rocky Mountain Wildflowers*. Houghton-Mifflin Co., Boston.

EWAN, JOSEPH A. 1950. *Rocky Mountain Naturalists*. Univ. of Denver Press, Denver, Colo:

HARRINGTON, H. D. 1954. *Manual of the Plants of Colorado*. Sage Books, Denver, Colo.

——————————. 1967. *Edible Native Plants of the Rocky Mountains*. Illustrated by Y. Matsumura. Univ. of New Mexico Press, Albuquerque.

——————————, and L. W. DURRELL. 1950. *Colorado Ferns and Fern Allies*. Colorado Agricultural Research Foundation, Colorado Agricultural and Mechanical College (now Colorado State University).

——————————————————. 1957. *How To Identify Plants*. Sage Books, Denver, Colo.

LONG, JOHN C. 1965. *Native Orchids of Colorado*. Denver Museum of Natural History Pictorial No. 16.

MARR, JOHN W. 1961. *Ecosystems of the East Slope of the Front Range in Colorado*. Univ. of Colorado Studies, Series in Biology, No. 8; 1-134.

MATSUMURA, YOSHIHARU, and H. D. HARRINGTON. 1955. *True Aquatic Vascular Plants of Colorado*. Tech. Bull. 57, Colorado Agricultural and Mechanical College.

McKEAN, WILLIAM T. (editor). 1956. *Winter Guide to Native Shrubs of the Central Rocky Mountains with Summer Key*. State of Colorado Game, Fish and Parks Dept., Denver, Colo.

McDOUGALL, W. B. 1964. *Grand Canyon Wild Flowers.* Museum of Northern Arizona, Flagstaff, Ariz.

―――――――――――――― , and HERMA BAGGLEY. 1956. *Plants of Yellowstone National Park.* Yellowstone Library and Museum Assn.

NELSON, RUTH ASHTON. 1969. *Handbook of Rocky Mountain Plants.* Dale Stuart King, Publisher, Tucson, Ariz.

OOSTING, HENRY J. 1958. *Study of Plant Communities.* 2d ed. W. H. Freeman and Co., San Francisco, Calif.

PESMAN, WALTER M. 1966. *Meet the Natives.* 7th ed. Botanic Gardens House, Denver, Colo.

PRESTON, RICHARD J., JR. 1940. *Rocky Mountain Trees.* Iowa State College Press, Ames, Iowa.

ROBERTS, HAROLD D., and RHODA ROBERTS. 1953. *Some Common Colorado Wild Flowers.* Denver Museum of Natural History Pictorial No. 8.

ROBERTS, RHODA, and RUTH ASHTON NELSON. 1957. *Mountain Wild Flowers of Colorado.* Denver Museum of Natural History Pictorial No. 13.

WEAVER, JOHN L., and FREDERIC E. CLEMENTS. 1929. *Plant Ecology,* McGraw-Hill Co., New York.

WEBER, WILLIAM A., 1972. *Rocky Mountain Flora. Colorado Associated University Press,* Boulder, Colo.

―――――――――――――― , in Madrono, Vol. 21, No. 6. Description of Mimulus gemmiparus Sp. Nov. New species.

WILLARD, BETTIE E., and CHESTER O. HARRIS. 1963. *Alpine Wild Flowers of Rocky Mountain National Park.* Rocky Mountain Nature Assn.

GENERAL INDEX

D

Daisy—127; aspen (fig. 154)—130; beautiful—128; black-headed—128; Coulter—130; cut-leaved—131; dryland—130; dwarf—130; early blue—130; Greenes—130; ox-eye—125; pale—130; pinnate-leaved—131; rockslide—130; spreading—128; subalpine—128; whiplash—130.

Daisies, fleabane—131.

Dandelion, common—141; burnt-orange—141; rock—141; tall false—141.

Danthonia—41.

Deathcamas, mountain—47.

Delphinium—68.

Deschampsia—41.

Descurania—72.

Disporum—47.

Dock, curly—57; Mexican—57.

Dodecatheon (fig. 119)—101.

Dogbane family—103.

Dogwood family—96.

Dogwood, red-osier—96.

Douglas-fir—39.

Draba—72.

Draba—72; golden—72; shiny—72; showy—72; twisted pod—72; white-flowered—72; yellow—72.

Dragonhead, American—110.

Dropseed, pine—42.

Dryad, mountain (figs. 82 and 83)—79.

Dryas (figs. 82 and 83)—79.

Dryopteris—37.

Duckweed family—44; star—44.

E

Easter-daisy—125.

Echinocactus—92.

Elaeagnaceae—92.

Elder, redberried (fig. 149)—119.

Eleocharis—44.

Elephantella (fig. 143)—116.

Elodea—40.

Elymus—42.

Engelmann spruce (fig. 9)—20.

Epilobium—93.

Equisetaceae—37.

Equisetum—37.

Ericaeceae—96.

Erigeron—127-131.

Eriogonum—56.

Eriophorum—44.

Eritrichium (fig. 131)—107.

Erodium—88.

Erysimum—72.

Erythronium (fig. 27)—47.

Euphorbia—88.

Euphorbiaceae—88.

Evening-primrose family—92; cut-leaf—95; Nuttall—95; stemless—95; yellow—95.

Evening-primrose—93.

Evening star, many-flowered—91; showy—91; white—91.

Everlasting, pearly—139.

F

Fairybells—47.

Fairy slipper (fig. 34)—49.

Fairy trumpet—105.

False-dandelion, tall—141.

Families of plants—34-142.

Felwort, marsh—102.

Fern, brittle—35; family—34; grass-leaved—37; holly—35; lip—37; oak—37; parsley—35; wood 37.

Fescue—40.

Fescue Tribe—40.

Festuca—40.

Festuceae—40.

Figwort family—110; lanceleaf—117; mountain—116; western—117.

Fir, subalpine—39; Douglas—39.

Fireberry hawthorn—82.

Fireweed (fig. 102)—93; broadleaved—93.

Flax, blue (fig. 97)—88; family—88; Lewis—88.

Fleabane, arctic (fig. 156)—130; bitter—131; daisies—131; spearleaf—131; trailing—130.

Flower, parts of— Fig. 2 of Glossary.

Forest, climax—24; Douglas-fir—17; Engelmann spruce-subalpine fir—20; fire—23; frontier—20; lodgepole—17; lodgepole—Douglas-fir—17; mixed—23; ponderosa pine—17.

Forget-me-not, alpine (fig. 131)—107.

Four-o'clock family—58; wild—58.

Foxtail—42; alpine—42; short-awned—42.

Fragaria—79.

Frasera—102.

Frontier forest—20.

Fumariaceae—70.

Fumitory family—70.

G

Gaillardia—131.

Gaillardia (fig. 157)—131.

Galium—119.

Gaultheria—98.

Gayfeather—139.

Gayophytum—93.

Gentian, arctic (fig. 125)—102; Bigelow—102; dwarf rose—103; family—101; fragrant—102; marsh—103; moss—102; one-flowered—103; Parry (fig. 124)—102; perennial fringed—102; Rocky Mountain fringed (fig. 123)—102; Rocky Mountain pleated—102; rose—103; star—102.

Gentiana—102, 103.

Gentianaceae—101.

Geraniaceae—86.

Geranium—86, 88.

Geranium—86; family—86; Fremont—86; Richardson—88.

Geum—79.

Gilia—105.

Gilia—105; skyrocket—105.

Ginseng family—95.

Globeflower (fig. 55)—63.

Globemallow, scarlet—89.

Glyceria—41.

Gnaphalium—139.

Gold buttons—131.

Gold-bloom saxifrage—75.

Gold-tongue owlclover—116.
Golden aster—131.
Golden banner—85.
Golden-eye—131.
Golden smoke—70.
Goldenglow—136.
Goldenrod—136; dwarf—136; giant—136; smooth —136.
Goldenweed—136; alpine—136; Parry—136.
Goodyera—51.
Gooseberry-currant—77.
Gooseberry family—77; mountain—77.
Goosefoot family—57.
Grama grass (fig. 22)—40.
Gramineae—40.
Grapeferns—34.
Grass, grama—40; family—40; see list—40-42.
Grasses, list of—40-42.
Grindelia—131.
Grossulariaceae—77.
Groundsel—133; Bigelow—134; lambstongue— 135.
Groundpine—38.
Grouseberry—98.
Gumweed, mountain—131.
Gymnocarpium—37.

H

Habenaria—51.
Hackelia—107.
Hairgrass—41.
Haloragaceae—95.
Haplopappus—136.
Harbouria—95.
Harebell, alpine—120; mountain (fig. 150)—120; Parry—120.
Hawksbeard, alpine—141.
Hawkweed, slender—141; white-flowered—141.
Hawthorn, fireberry—82.
Heath family—96.
Helianthella—138.
Helianthus—138.
Helictotrichon—41.
Hemlock-parsley—96.
Heracleum—95.
Heuchera—77.
Hieracium—141.
Hippuris—95.
Hollyfern, mountain—35.
Hollygrape, creeping—70.
Hollyhock, wild—89.
Holodiscus—81.
Honeysuckle—119; family—119; involucred—119.
Hordeae—42.
Hordeum—42.
Horsemint (fig. 137)—110.
Horsetail family—37; smooth—37.
Horseweed—142.
Huckleberry, broom—98.
Hydrangea family—78.
Hydrangeaceae—78.
Hydrocharitaceae—40.
Hydrophyllaceae—106.
Hydrophyllum—106.
Hymenoxys—133.
Hypericaceae—91.
Hypericum—91.

I

Indian-hemp—103.
Indian paintbrush—113.
Ipomopsis—105.
Iridacease—49.
Iris—49.
Iris—49; family—49; Rocky Mountain (fig. 32) —49.
Isoëtaceae—38.
Isoëtes—38.
Iva—142.

J

Jacobs ladder, subalpine (fig. 128)—105; western —105.
Jamesia—78.
Jamesia—78.
Juncaceae—44.
Juncaginaceae—39.
Juncus, see list—44.
Junegrass—41.
Juniper—39; dwarf—39; Rocky Mountain (fig. 3) —39.
Juniperus—39.

K

Kalmia—98; bog (fig. 112)—98.
Kings crown (fig. 73)—74.
Kinnikinnic (figs. 111 and 111a)—98.
Kittentail—117, alpine—117.
Knotweed, dooryard—57.
Knotweeds—57.
Kobresia—43.
Koeleria—41.
Koenigia—57.

L

Labiatae—109.
Ladies-tresses—51.
Lady fern, alpine—35; common—35.
Ladyslipper, yellow (fig. 35)—49; brownie—51.
Ladysthumb, water—57.
Lambsquarters—58.
Lappula—107.
Larkspur—68; mountain—68; Nelson—68; sub-alpine—68; western—68.
Laurel—98; bog—98.
Leguminosae—84.
Lemna—44.
Lemnaceae—44.
Lentibulariaceae—117.
Lepidium—72.
Lesquerella—72.
Leucocrinum—47.
Leucopoa—41.
Lewisia—58.
Liatris—139.
Lichens—23; crustose—23; foliose—23; leafy—23.
Ligusticum—96.
Liliaceae—46.
Lilium—47.

157

P

Pachystima—89.
Paintbrush, Indian—113; narrow-leaved—115; northern—115; rosy—115; scarlet—115; short-flowered—115; western yellow—115; Wyoming—115.
Papavera—70.
Papaveraceae—70.
Parnassia—77.
Parnassia, fringed—77.
Parnassus, grass of—77.
Paronychia—61.
Parrotfeather—95.
Parsley, alpine—96; mountain—96; whiskbroom—95.
Parsnip, cow—95; family—95.
Pasqueflower, American (fig. 56)—67.
Pea family—84; golden—85.
Pearly everlasting—139.
Pearlwort, arctic—61.
Pedicularis—116.
Pedicularis—116, 117; alpine—117; Grays—116.
Pediocactus—92.
Pennycress—72.
Penstemon—113.
Penstemon, clustered—113; dark—113; large clustered—113; low—113; sidebells—113; tall oneside—113.
Peppergrass—72.
Petasites—141.
Phacelia—106.
Phalarideae—42.
Phleum—40.
Phlox—105.
Phlox family—103; tufted—105.
Physocarpus—82.
Picea—39.
Pinaceae—38.
Pine—38; family—38; limber—38; lodgepole—38; ponderosa—38; seedlings of—23.
Pinedrops—99.
Pinesap—99.
Pink family—60; mountain—61.
Pink plumes—81.
Pinus—38.
Pipsissewa (fig. 110)—96.
Plagiobothrys—109.
Plant succession—23.
Plantaginaceae—119.
Plantago—119.
Plantain, common—119; family—119; Tweedy—119.
Poa—40, 41.
Podagrostis—42.
Poison-hemlock—96.
Poison-ivy, western—88.
Polemoniaceae—103.
Polemonium—105.
Polemonium, honey—105; leafy—105.
Polygonaceae—54.
Polygonum—57.
Polypodiaceae—34.
Polypodium—35.
Polypody, western—35.
Polystichum—35.
Pondlily, yellow—61.
Pondweed family—39.

Pondweeds—39.
Popcorn flower—109.
Poppy, alpine—70; family—70.
Populus—51, 52.
Portulacaceae—58.
Potamogeton—39.
Potato family—110.
Potentilla—81.
Prenanthes—142.
Pricklypear, plains (fig. 99)—92.
Pricklypoppy—70.
Primrose, alpine—99; fairy (fig. 115)—99; family—99; Parry (figs. 116 and 117)—99.
Primula—99.
Primulaceae—99.
Prince's pine (fig. 110)—96.
Prunella—110.
Prunella—110.
Prunus—84.
Pseudocymopterus—96.
Pseudotsuga—39.
Pteridium—35.
Pterospora (fig. 114)—99.
Puccoon, many-flowered—107; narrow-leaf—107.
Pulsatilla (fig. 56)—67.
Purple fringe (fig. 129)—106.
Purshia—82.
Purslane family—58.
Pussytoes—139; Rocky Mountain—139; showy—139.
Pussy willow—53; silver—53.
Pyrola—96.
Pyrola—96; bog (fig. 107)—96; green-flowered—96; one-sided—96; star-flowered (figs. 108 and 109)—96.

Q

Quackgrass, false—42.
Quillwort family—38.
Quillworts—38.

R

Rabbitbrush, dwarf—138.
Ragwort—133; arrowleaf—134; rock—135; saffron—136; toothed—134; western golden—135.
Rameschia—96.
Ranunculaceae—63.
Ranunculus—66.
Raspberry, boulder (fig. 81)—82; wild red—82.
Ratibida—136.
Rattlesnake-plantain, western—51.
Rattlesnakeroot—142.
Red-cedar, western (fig. 3)—17.
Redtop—41; Idaho—41; Ross—42; winter—41.
Reedgrass—42; Canadian—42; plains—42; purple 42; Scribner—42.
Rhamnaceae—89.
Rhus—88.
Ribes—77, 78.
Ricegrass—42; little—42; littleseed—42; rough-leaf—42.
Rockbrake, American—35.
Rockcress—71.
Rockjasmine (fig. 118)—101.
Rocky Mountain juniper—17.
Rorippa—72.

INDEX TO LOCALITIES

(See the map on pp. 166-67 for assistance in locating
these areas.)

ADMINISTRATION

Rocky Mountain National Park is administered by the National Park Service, U.S. Department of the Interior. A superintendent, whose address is Estes Park, Colo. 80517, is in immediate charge.

THE DEPARTMENT OF THE INTERIOR

As the Nation's principal conservation agency, the Department of the Interior has basic responsibilities for water, fish, wildlife, mineral, land, park, and recreational resources. Indian and Territorial affairs are other major concerns of America's "Department of Natural Resources." The Department works to assure the wisest choice in managing all our resources so each will make its full contribution to a better United States — now and in the future.

Front cover: Colorado columbine, with aspen in background, by Ted and Lois Matthews.

Inside front cover: Alpine view on Trail Ridge by author; hiker on Ute Trail by Robert Haines.

Back cover: Indian paintbrush.

PHOTO CREDITS

Inside back cover and back cover by Guy Burgess; figs. 16, 17, 19, 20, 22, 24, 25, 29, 34, 40, 41, 42, 53, 57, 69, 76, 78, 79, 82, 85, 86, 92, 93, 94, 96, 100, 103, 106, 111, 114, 115, 125, 151, 153, 159, 165, and 166 by author; figs. 18, 58, 71, 73a, 87, 91a, 99, 112, 133, 134, 136, 140, 158, and 161 by Richard A. Wilcox; figs. 21, 39, 46, and 123 by Robert Rothe; figs. 23, 70, 132, 137, and 149 by Wayne Alcorn; figs. 26, 32, 33, 43, 47, 56, 62, 77, 84, 101, 104, 107, 108, 110, 113, 120, 121, 124, 128, 130, 135, 138, 139, 142, 143, 148, 163, and 164 from Harold Roberts Collection, University of Colorado; figs. 27, 44, 50, 55, 72, 102, 119, 150, and 157 by Ted and Lois Matthews; figs. 28, 35, 37, 38, 66, 67, 68, 73, 80, 81, 95, 116, 126, 127, 129, 141, 145, 146, 160, 162, and 172 by Robert Haines; figs. 30, 45, 48, 49, 51, 52, 54, 60, 61, 64, 65, 74, 75, 83, 88, 89, 90, 91, 97, 98, 105, 117, 118, 131, 144, 147, 154, 155, 156, 167, 170, 171, 173, and 174 by Bettie Willard; fig. 31 by E. H. Rogers; fig. 36 by Richard A. DeLong; fig. 59 by John L. Colyn; fig. 63 by Tom D. Thomas; figs. 109 and 122 by Jack Dreibus; and fig. 169 by Dorothy Leake.

PRODUCTION CREDITS

Production Supervision: Galley & Associates, Inc.
Design: Les Hays Studios
Typography: Priesman Graphics
 (Century Schoolbook, News Gothic)
Color Separations, Assembly, Plates: Orent Graphic Arts, Inc.
Lithography: Omaha Printing Co.
Binding: Precision Bindery

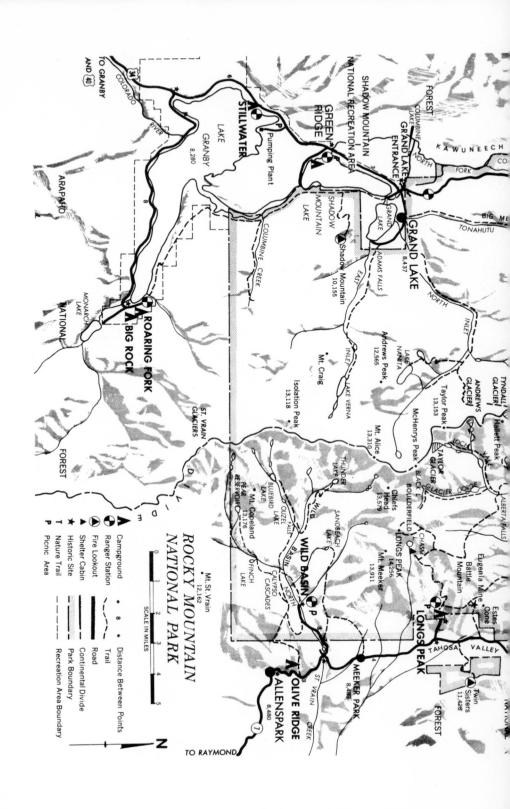

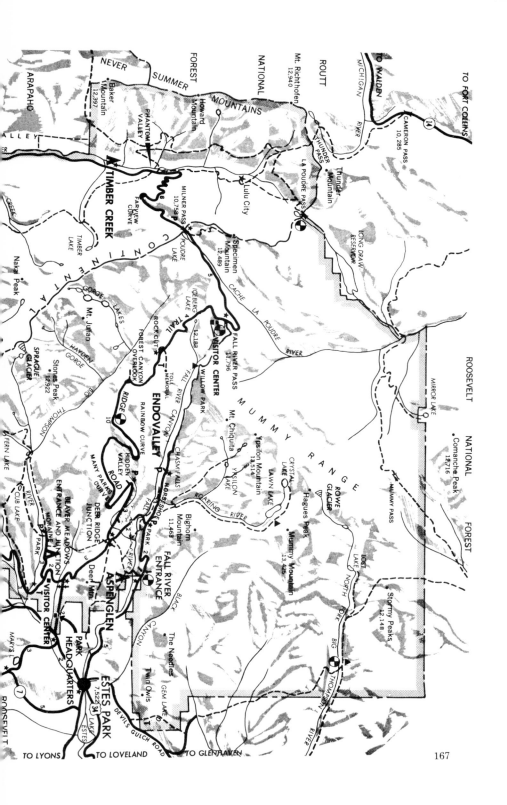

167

*Rocky Mountain National Park
is a unique resource
for inquiry into the human condition.
In it are exemplified
the elements and forces
and balances out of which
man himself is made,
and out of which
he spins his cities
and society and culture.
Everything man is, or builds,
is "nature" before it is anything else.*

*Ranger-naturalists explain
to park visitors some of nature's laws.
If we, who are a part of
nature, are to manipulate
the materials of nature
toward our uniquely human ends
and do so with creative
rather than destructive consequences
for ourselves and for our world,
then we must understand
and work within these laws.
The child who would learn
this lesson must approach it
with the idea that he,
himself, is as much a part
of the natural world —
as subject to its laws —
as are the trees,
the mountains, and the seas.*